I AM AN AMERICAN

A Story of Socialism, Communism, and Freedom's Last Stand

MIKLOS RADVANYI

FREILING
PUBLISHING

Published by Freiling Publishing, a division of Freiling Agency, LLC.

P.O. Box 1264
Warrenton, VA 20188

www.FreilingPublishing.com

ISBN: 978-1-956267-21-1

Printed in the United States of America

Table of Contents

Introduction

The Making of a True Refugee

A TRUE REFUGEE is a nonconformist from a country rotted by corruption to the core on a very personal journey of moral purification and enlightened self-fulfillment.

The nation of my birth has gone completely mad, politically and morally, because of the so-called Treaty of Trianon of 1920, in which Hungary lost two-thirds of its territory and two-thirds of its population. In the last hundred years, the resulting national trauma has produced unimaginable absurdities that have turned successive Hungarian societies into unbelievably hateful and immoral communities.

Between the two world wars, Hungarian politics went from unsuccessfully trying to stabilize a mutilated state to becoming a revanchist country of insane destruction under the chauvinistic slogan of taking the lost territories and peoples back by force. Again, the result of Hungary's so-called elite's cockamamie foreign policy was the military occupation of the country by the Red Army that lasted 45 years and the imposition of a Soviet-style communist dictatorship.

For starters, the Hungarian Communists who survived Stalin's relentless purges in Moscow returned to avenge the overthrow of their short-lived Council Republic in 1919. When the communist terror led to the death of almost all who dared to stand in their way, the people revolted in October of 1956. Their revenge was almost as bloody and ruthless as the reign of the Hungarian Stalin, Matyas Rakosi.

Again, the Red Army intervened and restored order by killing and raping indiscriminately. The Kremlin's new Gauleiter was named Janos Kadar, a true believer in the redeeming qualities of communism without any particular attraction to Soviet/Russian culture. He reigned for 30+ years over a nation whose mood was likened by many to a volcano that refused to erupt.

The withdrawal of the Red Army from Hungary in the spring of 1990, opened the door for the 10 million Hungarians to build a better democratic future for themselves and their posterity. The United States government and I were optimistic about the future of the country. Congress passed the SEED Act, which stood for Support Eastern European Democracy, under the able leadership of Congressman Christopher (Chris) Cox of California. Hungarian wannabe politicians crowded the hallways of congressional office buildings on both sides of the Capitol. Offers to assist with Hungary's transition were rejected by everybody with the rationale that only Hungarians could properly understand what the Hungarian people really wanted. Many newly minted politicians went even further. They loudly declared that after getting rid of the Soviet occupation, they would categorically refuse to become a colony of the United States of America or Western Europe.

Having lived in Hungary for 20 years, I knew the Hungarian mental illness of eponymous hatred of anything foreign as well as the Hungarian people's cynical and immoral logic would surely lead the way to another national catastrophe. As a former refugee who escaped Hungary in January 1973 and defying a long prison sentence and even the death penalty if caught, I recently returned to find a nation even more desperate and hopeless than when I left the country. A single political party has reigned unchallenged for the last 11 years like under the one-party rule of the old Communist party. Corruption has been all over the country. Citizenship has become a mere tool in the hands of the ruling FIDESZ party to maintain its fraudulent two-thirds majority in the Parliament. Close to one million young Hungarians have left the country to various lands of the European Union. As in the past hundred years, Hungary is sinking in its self-generated mud of stagnation and regression.

At the end of July 2021, I walked through the shopping district around Vaci street. The windows of most shops were boarded up, clearly abandoned for good. The downtown hotels were practically empty of foreign tourists. On the streets, I saw people walking with apathetic faces. Hopelessness regarding the future was everywhere. The next morning, I boarded a train to Vienna, Austria. The distance from the Hungarian capital of Budapest is about two hours, yet what a contrast! Cleanliness, order, bustling streets, overbooked hotels, shops full of potential buyers, and mostly happy faces. The difference between the mentality of a former Communist country and the mentality of a nation that was spared the soul-killing life of the Soviet occupation is indescribable.

Three days later, I returned to Budapest, Hungary, by train. On the train, the announcer greeted the passengers in Hungarian, German, and English. The Hungarian greeting was accompanied by a warning that admonished the Hungarian-speaking passengers to pay close attention to their belongings and never lose sight of them. The additional warning was not repeated in the other two languages. This small episode told the entire story. What is normal in Hungary is abnormal outside of the country.

This book was written with all of these thoughts in mind. It was also written because I love the United States of America more than I love my life. What I have witnessed in the last five years has filled my mind and my heart with deep sorrow. A miniscule minority that has historically contributed very little to America's greatness has decided to destroy the legacy of 240 years in order to rule it.

Employing a language that is extremely racist, fanatically hateful, and bigotedly fallacious, this miniscule minority is determined to install a completely false reality as a fraudulent ideology across the nation. I would like to consider my book as a warning against the United States of America's descent into the destructive and Stalinist-like idiocy of this minority. The

American people must fight against this attempted degeneration of the American spirit with all their might. I am certain that together we will defeat this monstrous psychopathy and racial totalitarianism of this miniscule minority.

1

A Global Perspective

BEYOND THE TWO world wars, the 20th century will surely be remembered as the centennial of the refugees. The 21st century has already manifested itself as the golden age for uncontrollable mass migration from utterly failed, underdeveloped as well as developing countries to the developed countries of Europe and the United States of America. This attempt at inverse colonization has resulted in two turbulent decades in the 21st century across the globe.

According to the Vienna Yearbook of Population Research, "Momentous changes are going on in Europe. Immigrants are arriving in unprecedented numbers, and they are re-shaping the structures and composition of the European population. [...] Populations are becoming much more diversified in their languages, ethnic groups and religions. Eventually, if recent trends continue, the self-identity and even the physical appearance of Europe's people will be changed." Specifically, Muslim integrations and assimilations have been unmitigated failures throughout the European continent. More alarmingly, Muslim children and women across Europe have been subjected to

Taliban-like sharia rules, indoctrination, and intra-violence by extremist Muslim preachers as well as politically motivated agitators.

On the other side of the Atlantic Ocean, the Age of Mass Migration has become a major political issue. The Democrat Party champions open borders, while the Republican Party calls for legally controlled immigration. The Democrats argue that the United States of America has always been a nation of immigrants, while the Republicans counter with attacking the blatant illegality of uncontrollable mass migration as well as the intentionally confusing and ideologically fallacious narrative about political asylum versus unbridled illegal economic migration.

More importantly, while most of the arguments on both sides of the aisle have focused on the economic impact of mass migration, the political consequences to the constitutional civilization of the United States of America have been coming more and more to the forefront of the national division. Finally, the ubiquitous cultural differences between the illegal immigrants and the natives have only exacerbated the already existing existential differences across the nation. To add insult to injury, these illegal newcomers, encouraged by the ideology of multiculturalism and neo-racism charges of "White Supremacy" as well as "Systematic and Institutionalized Racism," are refusing in increasing numbers to assimilate into the political, economic, cultural, and legal order of the country.

On January 20, 2021, Acting Department of Homeland Security Secretary David Pekoske sent an operational memorandum to the leadership of the U.S. Immigration and Customs Enforcement (ICE) and Citizenship and Immigration Service (CIS). This ill-conceived memorandum instructed both agencies to ignore the law as referenced in the Immigration and Nationality Act (INA), a law duly enacted by Congress and signed by then President Lyndon B. Johnson in 1965. Commonly known as the Hart-Celler Act after its two main Democrat sponsors, Senator Philip A. Hart of Michigan and Representative Emanuel Celler of New York, this law overhauled America's immigration system during a time of great global instability.

After the Pekoske memo and in his boundless stupidity, on April 19, 2021, the newly elected Doofus-in-Chief of the United States of America President Joe Biden ordered all departments of the executive branch to change the terms used to describe immigration matters, including how to refer to those who enter the country illegally. According to Fox News, the administration order came in the form of memos sent to the leaders of Immigration and Customs Enforcement (ICE) and Customs and Border Protection (CBP) and was first reported by the Washington Times. Accordingly, "Alien" was changed to "Noncitizen" or "Migrant." "Alienage" was changed to "Non Citizenship." "Unaccompanied Alien Children" were to be called "Noncitizen Unaccompanied Children." "Undocumented Alien" and "Illegal Alien" were changed to "Undocumented Noncitizen" and "Undocumented Individual or Migrant." "Assimilation" changed to "Integration or Civil Integration," and "Immigrant Assimilation" became "Immigrant Integration."

Of course, the distinction between integration and assimilation is crucial from a political and cultural standpoint. Integration means a process of incorporation as an equal into society while preserving the cultural, linguistic otherness of the individual. Assimilation, on the other hand, means a process through which individuals and groups of differing heritages acquire basic habits, attitudes, and ways of life by embracing the culture of the welcoming society in its totality. Clearly, a big difference. By talking about integration and not assimilation, the Biden administration and the Democrat Party signal to every newcomer, whether he or she is a legal or illegal immigrant, that they do not have to fully become an integral part of American society. They can maintain their separate non-American status.

Denying realities by abusing the English language to justify the great lie of humanistic values and in order to gain authoritarian political as well as economic powers, Department of Homeland Security's head Alejandro Mayorkas has canceled fines for illegal immigrants who refuse to leave and will grant amnesty for all fines already imposed by the Trump administration. The Biden administration's willful ignorance of reality has been manifested fully by the vice president's intractable refusal to even pay a visit to the southern border. Adding another false ideological insult to the already existing massive legal injury, the above mentioned Secretary of the Department of Homeland Security has declared that the agents of various departments and agencies responsible to uphold and implement the law regarding illegal immigration shall be forbidden to take into custody or arrest any illegal immigrant inside any courthouse.

For good measure and to demonstrate that the president thinks most Americans' intellectual levels do not exceed his idiocy, he grandiloquently stated, "The policy of my administration is to protect national and border security, address the humanitarian challenges at the southern border, and ensure public health and safety." Not being satisfied with these monstrous lies, his executive order continues, "We must also adhere to due process of law as we safeguard the dignity and well-being of all families and communities. My administration will reset the policies and practices for enforcing civil immigration laws to align enforcement with these values and priorities."

There is nothing in President Biden's high-flying declaration about protecting Americans against the criminal elements among the waves of illegal immigrants. Yet, since January 20, 2021, Americans across the United States of America have witnessed a huge increase in the criminal activities of Central and South American gangs, most prominently by the Sinaloa Cartel and MS-13, who have used illegal weapons indiscriminately and ruthlessly against innocent American citizens. Regrettably, the Biden administration and the Democrat Party see all of this as business as usual. Americans are murdered, and no one is doing anything about it. On the contrary, foreign criminals are rewarded with false humanistic impunity.

For any card-carrying member of the Democrat Party, such an outrageous lie to replace facts with a false reality should be a moment of truth. This palpable verbal prostitution of words, terms, and definitions in order to serve a nakedly political purpose can only lead to a national catastrophe. President Biden's demented justification to disguise his party's power-expansionist designs behind false humanitarian reasoning is simply evil. Even in his pre-dementia condition, he has never been accused of being smart. Him not grasping the enormous tragedy that his idiotic policies will surely create is unbelievable. If his and his party's psychopathic drive is not stopped, it will definitely result in the collapse of American civilization and the Constitutional Republic.

Thus, instead of striving to understand each other, wokeism with its neo-racism, neo-segregationalism, identity politics, cancel culture, Critical Race Theory, etc., has misleadingly empha-sized stereotypes, misunderstandings, unreal expectations, and destruction of relationships in place of relationship building and finding commonality among cultures within American society. Equally dishearteningly, while American society has been built on tolerance for two-and-a-half centuries, wokeism has expelled humanism from its hate-filled rhetoric.

However, Blacks, Whites, Hispanics, Asians, and other ethnic and religious communities have had historical communalities beyond race and religion because they have shared common family as well as social values. They have existed side by side for almost 250 years and have shared a common language, names, roots, education, etc. With only a few exceptions, Whites have great respect for Blacks. Hispanics, and Asians for having retained the positive aspects of their traditions and vice versa. The United States of America has always been proud of its cultural diversity by having emphasized the importance of the good and the bad that the nation has witnessed through its glorious history. Successive federal and state governments have always taken very seriously their duty of preserving all cultures together. No other nation on earth has more museums, national monuments, and protected grounds dedicated to all races, ethnic groups, and religions than the United States of America.

Naturally, neither Americans or Europeans must allow these newcomers to redefine American and European civilization, culture, and country. More specifically, the new and completely unfounded accusation of white supremacy cannot go unchallenged. Instead of being ashamed of "Whiteness" and remaining cowardly silent, Europeans and Americans alike must be proud of and loud about the revolutionary ideas and enormous accomplishments of their civilization in the general progress of the world.

Simultaneously, both Europeans and Americans must emphasize that Western civilization has always striven to be inclusive by uniting and not dividing mankind. Equally importantly,

Western civilization has been founded on the universality of love and kindness of the Old and New Testaments as opposed to the neo-racist hatred of Black Lives Matter and Antifa, among others, their fraudulent race-baiting, and the resulting irrationally mindless destruction. Finally, "Whiteness" cannot and should not be allowed to become the modern boogeyman of jealousy and power as well as money-hungry minority psychopaths who have historically been devoid of any civilization, proper education, ethical culture, and positive attitudes to productive life.

Of course, no civilization, culture, or political system is perfect. However, the longevity of Western civilization is proof of the legitimacy and relevancy of Western identity. In turn, this Western identity also means that Europeans as well as Americans must embrace their past, present, and future with pride and without any hesitation. History binds and does not divide. Western civilization and Western identity have never been limited by color, race, or ethnicity. Whites, Blacks, Orientals, etc., are equal in this highly successful civilization and ethical world. As Martin Luther King stated, people should be judged not by the color of their skin but by the content of their character.

Yet, more generally, these chaotic two decades of the 21st century will surely remain a completely unsolvable riddle as long as the real impacts of four momentous events—the sudden collapse of the Soviet Union in 1991, the stealthy rise of the People's Republic of China, the devastating impact of the Chinese/Wuhan coronavirus-induced pandemic, and the recurring failures of Europe's and America's domestic and international policies—are not understood correctly.

Pursuant to the prevalent view in the United States of America, the breakup of the Soviet Union was the result of the inferiority of the Marxist-Leninist-Stalinist ideology as a functioning political, economic, and social regime vis-a-vis the Western political culture. From the Kremlin's perspective, the United States of America and its allies, especially in Europe, had precious little to do with the demise of the Soviet Union. According to the Russian narrative, the Soviet Union was destroyed from within by the Communist Party elite which is a fundamental contradiction in perspectives that is at the heart of the historic confusion of the last three decades. On the one hand, there is the image of the triumphant West. On the other hand, there is the picture of a completely defeated East. Consequently, what appeared to be a decisive victory over the "Evil Empire" from Washington, D.C., was seen as a voluntary abandonment of the so-called Cold War in Moscow.

The new Russia clearly looked for its place in the changing world. In order to be integrated into the just emerging new world order, its government, headed by an emotionally unstable alcoholic Boris Nikolayevich Yeltsin, was willing to accept the White House's lead. However, the imposition of democracy and a free-market economy have run into the impenetrable twin walls of the ossified mentality of the old communist bureaucracy and the all-pervasive corruption that have plagued and rotted Russian societies to the core from the onset of the Mongol rule after the Kievan Rus and beyond. Thus, the last decade of the 20th century proved that it is easier to erase the Soviet Union with its quasi-Communist ideology from the Russian minds than to change the ancestral mentality of the majority of the Russian people. At that time, neither the Russian politicians nor the political leaders of the West fully comprehended that it is not enough to defeat an entrenched and counterproductive political system. In order to change the minds of the people, the entire culture of a nation must be transformed. For this reason, the people should have been involved and should have been made a part of the great political, economic, social, and cultural transformation. Clearly, nonparticipation creates confusion, misunderstanding, apathy, cynicism, and rejection. In one word, it leads to failure.

On the other side of the globe, President George H.W. Bush attempted to balance two seemingly contradictory concepts. In order to strengthen the cohesion of the "Free World," he declared the vision of "Europe whole and free." In his speech on May 31, 1989, in Mainz, Germany, he assured the crowd that the United States of America was ready and willing to lead a United Europe that was based on the shared values of democracy, freedom, and prosperity. Since it was impossible to establish a United Europe without the cooperation of the Soviet Union, President Bush sat down with then Soviet leader Mikhail Sergeyevich Gorbachev on December 2, 1989, off the coast of Malta.

The Malta Summit officially put an end to the Cold War. However, beyond the declaratory good intentions of striving to build a new relationship between East and West, very little of strategic value was accomplished at Malta. In fact, President Bush's hybrid approach of providing American leadership in the post-Cold War world has proven to be misguided. Also adapted by his successor, President William (Bill) J. Clinton, this solution has not eliminated the old conflict between the dominant European power in the East and the rest of the continent in the West. On the contrary, with the emergence of the new Russian President Vladimir Vladimirovich Putin at the end of the century, this dualistic solution merely aggravated the confrontation between the less developed Eastern and the significantly more developed Western parts of Europe.

Adding strategic insult to foreign policy incompetence by the Clinton administration, President Clinton stated that his administration would use the so-called "Peace Dividend from the End of the Cold War" to enhance domestic spending, mainly in the health and social security areas of the economy. Concurrently, the Clinton administration completely failed to formulate a coherent global foreign policy and set national strategic objectives for the present and the future.

No wonder then that under these forlorn conditions, American foreign policy was not coordinated either by the White House or the State Department. Instead, foreign policy was haphazardly franchised to several departments, various congressional committees, and even the institutions of higher education, such as Harvard, Yale, Princeton, Stanford, etc. Loaded at the time with so-called "Russia experts" who arrived in large numbers from the former Soviet Union, they spotted an opportunity to join the party in the new Russian Federation and try to enrich themselves and their universities by the Russian version of "Wild West Capitalism." Simultaneously, NATO's security strategy remained frozen in the obsolete goal of old-fashioned containment and the dead-end doctrine of Mutually Assured Distraction (MAD).

On January 20, 2009, an even more incompetent President Barack Obama was inaugurated. This community organizer, state senator, and rookie U.S. senator from the state of Illinois with no foreign policy experience at all went from the unrealistically stupid "Reset" to the strategically idiotic "Refreeze" Russian policy within his destructive eight years in office. Supported by the Secretary of State, Hillary Rodham Clinton, whose sole qualification for the job was her marital relationship to a former president, President Obama did a disservice to global and regional strategic interests of the United States of America and its allies across the globe. Thus, following the lackluster performance of the Clinton administration and the terrorist attacks of September 11, 2001, the general mediocrity of the George W. Bush presidency, combined with the professional incompetence and the moral ambiguity of the Obama administration, resulted in weakening the stability and peace upon which the post-World War II international system was founded.

In the meantime, both countries faced major domestic and foreign policy challenges. Moscow had to manage the international aftermath of the dissolution of the Soviet Union and the withdrawal of its troops from Eastern Europe and Afghanistan. Domestically, the reorganization of the government and the ensuing chaos as well as the heavy losses inflicted by the robber economy paved the way for the emergence of a new strongman in the Kremlin at the end of 1999. The history of the successive two decades under President-Prime Minister-President Vladimir Putin has contained more failures than successes. The Russian Federation is still a developing country waiting impatiently to progress. The form of government has reverted to outright dictatorship, the economy has continued being dependent on the export of raw materials, and the pervasiveness of rampant corruption as well as the degree of the people's immorality have remained legendary.

Clearly, the "New Russia" has proven to be a new sequel of the old despotic Tsarist Imperial Russia and its 20th century corpse, the Soviet Union. Presently, the Russian Federation with President Putin at the helm is a military dictatorship pared of excellence and devoid of liberty, tolerance, and humanism. As throughout its bloody history, the masses are enslaved and kept as close as possible to mental imbecility by the government propaganda. The dread of the people is matched step by step by the fear of the President and his entourage. This horrible mutual fearfulness increases exponentially with the rise of oppression and the corresponding rebelliousness of the people. Thus, instead of progressing toward democracy, Russia will remain a despotic and semi-feudal state that will continue to pose an enduring threat to the rest of Europe as well as the United States of America.

Domestically, American society has regressed into President Obama's deliberately induced and revoltingly atrocious political, ethnic, economic, religious, and race-based divisions. The over politicization of every aspect of American society has led to the emergence of all kinds of radical extremist groups and movements, such as Black Lives Matter, #MeToo, Antifa, Critical Race Theory, the Lincoln Project, and various partisan mobs espousing divergent, single-issue, political and social causes, such as gun control, climate change, illegal immigration, privacy rights, abortion, defunding the police, and attacking the judiciary, among others.

However, none of these groups and movements have been intellectually thoughtful or sincere. Generally speaking, they have been fraudulent and hastily improvised by the least educated and most excitable elements of American society, mostly with scant or no educational background at all. Assiduously encouraged and even incited by the Obama administration with its primitive slogan of "Fundamental Transformation" and an irresponsible media, Americans have become increasingly less confident and more skeptical of their government's ability to manage the domestic and foreign challenges facing their nation. As the driving force of President Obama's desired change at all cost, lawlessness has become the great passion that, combined with the ugly charge of racism, has put the nation into many artificially induced crises. Running for president with the frightening promise of continuing the Obama incompetence and chaos on the Democrat ticket, Hillary R. Clinton was soundly defeated by Republican Donald J. Trump, an outsider.

The four years that followed her defeat will surely enter the annals of American history as the vilest conspiracy against the constitutional order of the United States of America. The colossal enormity of the plan to delegitimize by the most ruthless use of unquestionably illegal means, including absolute lies and outrageous innuendos, the duly elected president of the United States of America could have originated only at the highest level of the White House, most probably by President Obama himself. Beyond the moral qualms about pursuing his personal vendetta to the detriment of the national interest, President Obama deliberately exacerbated every interaction between the Democrats and Republicans by reducing his hatred toward President Trump to the simplistic notion of "Us versus Them."

Moreover, President Obama's toxic policy of relativity has also intimated that the supporters of President Trump must only be defined in relation to the enlightened and virtuous Obama Democrats. Thus, having preemptively destroyed any possibility of nonpartisan unifying ideas and actions, President Obama, while still in office, embarked on destroying the principle of the rule of law too. Finally, in his primitive arrogance and hatred, he undoubtedly attempted to paralyze the incoming Trump administration. Consequently, "Trump bashing" has become both a national as well as an international pastime for all "America haters and critics."

The insinuation that President Trump beat the Democrat nominee because the former and his advisers colluded with the Kremlin only added malignant fuel to the sustained and vindictive political fire. After numberless millions of false media contributions and two impeachment proceedings, the Great Lie about the Russia Collusion turned out to be totally unfounded, essentially a hoax concocted by the Obama White House and carried out by his blindly loyal followers. The protracted Mueller investigation did not produce any evidence to the contrary. Yet, the real victims of the extreme weaponization of ideological differences have been the United States of America and its relationships with the rest of the world.

The China/Wuhan COVID-19 pandemic has added another major issue to the destructive polarization of American society. As a result, presidents, prime ministers, monarchs, and dictators across the globe must have concluded that the United States of America has become woefully unbalanced. With the inauguration of President Joseph (Joe) R. Biden, the domestic and foreign problems of America have only gotten more complex and numerous.

Meanwhile, the Wuhan Institute of Virology in China has conducted research on bat viruses in conjunction with the U.S. National Institute of Health (NIH) for many years on behalf of the Chinese military. To demonstrate the unbelievable naivete at best and the limitless idiocy of the NIH scientists, Congress, and the Executive Branch, the NIH has funded much of the Wuhan Institute's work with the justification that after the outbreak of SARS in 2002, more studies are needed to prevent another worldwide outbreak of bat-originated similar diseases.

A study published under the title "Discovery of a Rich Gene Pool of Bat SARS-Related Coronaviruses Provides New Insights into the Origin of SARS Coronavirus" revealed the discovery of three new viruses that have all shown a unique new characteristic—they all contained a "spike protein" that appeared to be particularly effective at grabbing on to a specific receptor in human lung cells known as an ACE2 receptor. The study clearly stated that these viruses could be very dangerous for humans and are under the control of the Chinese military.

When U.S. Embassy health and science officials went to Wuhan between 2017 and 2020 and met with Shi Zhengli (dubbed the "bat woman"), they were shocked by what they heard. According to Dr. Shi, the institute lacked enough properly trained technicians to safely operate their BSL-4 laboratory. The embassy officials' cables to Washington, D.C., did not trigger any action on the part of the American government. The same nonchalant and unprofessional bureaucratic approach was in full display on January 15, 2020, when a man of Chinese descent and a U.S. resident in his 30s arrived in Seattle from Wuhan.

Most probably fearing being labeled xenophobic in this politically correct city, a local health official by the name of Chris Bitters gave an optimistic opinion about the health of the Chinese individual, stating he was "in good condition and hospitalized out of an abundance of precaution and for short-term monitoring." His announcement was promptly followed by the CDC's assessment that the risk to the general public of this known first case was "low" because the Chinese individual was admitted to the hospital early and had been "very cooperative" with health authorities.

Washington State Secretary of Health John Wiesman doubled down on praising the Chinese man, "I'm grateful that the man who tested positive for the virus acted so quickly to seek treatment. Because of that, we were able to isolate him away from the public, and these actions gave us a head start. [...] All this work means that we believe the risk to the public is low." Uh-oh! This was mindless political correctness in full display by bureaucratic naivete, incompetence, and political correctness with its highly destructive character.

On January 11, 2020, just four days before the Chinese citizen's arrival in Seattle, Chinese officials reported that the total number of confirmed cases had jumped to 324 with the bulk of them being in the epicenter and ground zero of the COVID-19 epidemic—the Hubei province. Additional confirmed cases were reported in quick succession in Beijing, Shanghai, Tianjin, Guangdong, Zhejiang, Henan, and Chongqing. At the same time, Wuhan health authorities admitted that 15 medical personnel in the city had contracted the virus, an indirect confirmation that the virus was spreading by human transmission.

There is overwhelming evidence that Washington state health officials were completely oblivious to the two main characteristics of Chinese culture—ingrained racism of the Han Chinese and their shameless lying. In direct contradiction to the Roman belief that the truth shall liberate you, the Chinese hold that lying is a virtue. Thus, throughout millennia and countless centuries, the enduring complaints of both natives and foreigners have been the boundless dishonesty of the people in general and their shameless cheating in dealings with other people, be it in business or production of goods. From time immemorial, Chinese traders have customarily put fraudulent brands and fake trademarks on their merchandise. Such deception has gone hand-in-hand with inferior quality and bribery designed to corrupt both wholesalers as well as retailers. Impressionable children and teenagers have been taught from an early age that cheating the "Hairy People", meaning all non-Han Chinese, is a virtue and should be a source of pride because of those people's inferiority to the racially as well as intellectually superior Chinese nation.

These and similar Chinese practices have been in full display throughout the COVID-19 pandemic. In addition to hoarding and then mislabeling various personal protection equipment (PPE) from all over the world, European countries discovered that masks supplied by China for inflated prices had little or no protective properties at all. The same applied to rapid test kits and the same fate has awaited N95 respirators, ventilators, and other medical supplies.

More recently, as the global race to produce COVID-19 vaccines has seriously gotten rolling, China has come up with the Sinovac and Sinopharm vaccines. In addition to not having been tested properly, both vaccines have underperformed in developing antibodies and in preventing infections and transmissions. Not to be deterred, China has embarked on developing two more vaccines, the CanSino Biologics as well as another, presently unnamed vaccine by Anhui Zhifei Longcom. Clearly, human lives mean nothing or precious little to the Chinese government and its licensed mercenaries when it comes to generating income by defrauding the gullible "Hairy People."

Thus, instead of supplying quality merchandise, the Chinese Communist Party has mounted a propaganda offensive to fortify its outrageous and hypocritical trade practices. A whole army of Chinese government spokespersons, headed by Zhao Lijian, a foreign ministry spokesman, has arrogantly berated everybody who dared question and criticize the sincerity and integrity of the Chinese Communist Party and its licensed and unlicensed distributors. This Chinese pushback has been coordinated centrally and is well financed. Objective and factual reporting has been labeled by China and their corrupted foreign journalists an "immoral slander."

The People's Republic of China's "Vaccine Diplomacy" has been extended to falsely state that the Pfizer vaccine is basically a killer developed by the evil Americans. With the surreptitious assistance of Facebook, Google, Instagram, Twitter, and LinkedIn, the Chinese government has spent hundreds of millions of dollars to denigrate Western-made vaccines and praise to high heaven the almost useless Chinese vaccines. Beijing has been so committed to this lying narrative that it stated it could not provide real data because the virus was already eradicated in the People's Republic of China, solely using their homemade vaccines.

Lying and cheating, these quintessentially Chinese characteristics, have been projected onto Beijing's foreign policy too. In the main, the Chinese Communist Party has not been looking for allies and alliances. President Xi Jinping, the newly minted Mao as the "Great Helmsman," and his colleagues in the Politburo have always been looking for countries whose leaders could be corrupted by money and thus rendered totally subservient to Chinese foreign policy by making them hopelessly addicted to and dependent on Chinese financial and economic largesse.

In Asia, the People's Republic of China has assumed the role of a ruthless bully, especially in the South China Sea, the

Malacca Strait, Taiwan, and the Senkaku Islands, also known by the Chinese name the Diaoyudao Islands. In Africa, the strategy of corrupting politicians has found an ample number of willing and receptive takers. In Europe, especially in Central and Eastern Europe, the Balkans, Greece, Italy, Spain, and France, Beijing has pursued a cautious bilateral financial and economic penetration strategy.

Contrary to Russia's objectives aimed at weakening or even splitting up the European Union, Beijing's goal is to gradually erode the alliance between the United States of America and its allies. Beijing's corrupt practices have also poisoned the orderly functioning of the United Nations and almost all of its specialized agencies. The People's Republic of China does not want partnerships; it aims at reforming the world to its own image and then dominating it.

The best and most recent illustration is the World Health Organization's (WHO) dysfunctional reaction to the outbreak of the China/Wuhan COVID-19 virus. The Organization's current director, General Dr. Tedros Adhanom Ghebreyesus, is not a medical doctor. Less an Ethiopian microbiologist and more a dedicated anti-democratic and anti-capitalist Marxist politician, he has been an incompetent and corrupt political hack throughout his undistinguishable political career. Having been the first non-physician at the helm of the WHO in the organization's history, in his previous incarnation, Dr. Tedros was a member of an oppressive dictatorship that repeatedly lied about three consecutive cholera outbreaks in Ethiopia. As Ethiopia's foreign minister between 2012 and 2016, he defended the regime's egregious human rights violations and its genocidal crimes in Ethiopia's largest region of Oromia in 2015 and the Amhara region in 2016.

No wonder this dork has a soft spot in his heart, mind, and pocket for the Communist regime in the People's Republic of China. After considerable hesitation, Dr. Tedros flew to Beijing on January 28, 2020, almost a month after Dr. Li Wenliang warned his colleagues and the larger public about an illness resembling severe acute respiratory syndromes (SARS). His professional warning did not remain unpunished. Shortly after appearing before the Public Security Bureau in Wuhan, he died.

Proving the security apparatus is more efficient than its medical community, many of his colleagues were arrested for speaking out against the politically motivated ignorance of the Chinese Communist Party. In spite of the rapidly growing vocal demand by more and more Chinese physicians, the WHO issued a statement on January 20, 2020, stating there has been "limited human-to-human transmission" of the coronavirus. For good measure, the WHO announcement added, "This is in line with experience with other respiratory illnesses and in particular with other coronavirus outbreaks." The WHO finally declared COVID-19 a global emergency on January 30, 2020.

President Trump rightly criticized the biased behavior of the WHO, stating, "The World Health Organization has been a disaster. Everything they've said was wrong. And they are China-centric. They agree with China, whatever China wants to do. So our country, perhaps foolishly in retrospect, has been paying $450 million a year to the World Health Organization." To illustrate the validity of President Trump's point, the May 8, 2020, edition of the German magazine *Der Spiegel* wrote that the WHO's January 14, 2020, statement was made upon the personal request of President Xi, who wanted to conceal from the world the extent of the COVID-19 virus. To make matters worse, President Xi's wife, Peng Liyuan, happened to be a Goodwill Ambassador of the WHO.

However, this Chinese connection has been concealed from the public by the organization. On the WHO's website, Ms. Peng was listed as a singing star. *The Taiwan News* and *India World* also reported in unison that Chinese authorities did not stop international flights until the end of March, while it locked down all domestic traffic as early as the end of January 2020.

As of July 4, 2021, there have been about 215 million cases of COVID-19 worldwide. No doubt this number will rise exponentially in the coming years and perhaps decades. The death toll has spiked to over 4.5 million. Together, these events triggered by President Xi and his party's strategic intention to spread the novel coronavirus and thus to ensure the People's Republic of China would not be the only country to suffer significant political, financial, and economic hardships are indicative of the political as well as moral character of the regime.

Historically, all-encompassing power lust and corruption have been a destructive curse of all Chinese societies. Yet with the establishment of the People's Republic of China in 1949, political, economic, social, cultural, and moral corruption, driven by the monopoly of the Chinese Communist Party, has institutionalized lawlessness combined with the notion of political and legal impunity. Within this perfect storm, the abuse of power for personal ends has conquered all of the institutions of government, including party and administrative organizations, law enforcement, healthcare, education, and business. The political thaw that followed Mao Zhedong's death has only exacerbated the already destructive nature of prevalent corruption with Chinese characteristics.

As long as Chinese corruption has remained within the boundaries of the People's Republic, it has only been a relatively well-contained local phenomenon which has not risen to a significant international problem. However, with the disappearance of the Soviet Union and the independence of its oppressed satellites, the question of the quality of political and market liberalization has gained renewed importance for the United States of America as well as for its European allies.

However, more freedom throughout the former Soviet Empire has resulted in a marked increase in the level of corruption. According to a 2020 report by *Transparency International* which also includes all of the previous states within the Soviet sphere of influence, they have experienced "limited separation of powers, abuse of state resources for electoral purposes, opaque political party financing and conflict of interest." Coupled with limited judicial independence, minimal press freedom, and a lack of checks and balances among the three branches of government, these perfect storms have created a very similar kind of corruption that has always existed in the People's Republic of China.

In this context, the People's Republic of China has initiated the 16+1 Platform, also called the China-Central European Countries (China-CEEC) Summit in 2012. Ostensibly, it has been designed to further economic cooperation between Beijing and a collection of 11 European Union (EU) member states and 5 additional Balkan countries, namely Albania, Bosnia-Herzegovina, Bulgaria, Croatia, the Czech Republic, Estonia, Hungary, Latvia, Lithuania, Macedonia, Montenegro, Poland, Romania, Serbia, Slovakia, and Slovenia. While the establishment of the platform has predated the "Belt and Road Initiative" (BRI), the Chinese have viewed the 16+1 Platform format as a vehicle to strengthen bilateral relations with the participating states via investments in infrastructure, all kinds of technologies, and education.

Needless to say, corruption has been ripe concerning the $15.4 billion investment loan. It must also be noted that EU officials in Brussels have been increasingly critical of the 16+1 Platform. Mainly, they have been worried that China's real intentions are to undermine European unity in general and skew the

European Union's policies across Europe in favor of the People's Republic of China.

In this respect, Hungary has become the Chinese Trojan horse within NATO as well as the European Union. The Hungarian government, headed by Viktor Orban, has been a criminal organization from its inception, a political and business mafia more exactly. Having been elected in 2010 with a two-thirds majority in Parliament, Viktor Orban's party, the Alliance of Free Democrats (Hungarian acronyms: FIDESZ), has passed a new constitution, changed it nine times, distorted the legal system to their advantage, neutered the judiciary, installed a party hack as the chief prosecutor of the Republic, carried out the Gleichschaltung of education from kindergarten to the universities, and eliminated press freedom altogether. Concerning the People's Republic of China, the Orban regime has allowed the Chinese Communist Party to establish its European Spy Center in Budapest.

Lately, Viktor Orban personally agreed to build a huge campus of the Fudan University in Budapest with money borrowed from the Chinese. It is also to be erected by Chinese workers who will use Chinese building material exclusively. Also, the Hungarian government declared the establishment of the Fudan University strategically essential for the country, thus excluding the leadership of the capital city from any decision making, while taking absolute control over the entire project. The enormity of Viktor Orban's arrogance and corruption can be best illustrated by his regime's previous expulsion of the Central European University for its alleged ties to the Hungarian-born billionaire George Soros.

Even the COVID-19 pandemic has been used by Orban and his co-criminals to stuff their pockets with millions and millions of dollars. To accomplish this criminal feat, Hungary has purchased the Chinese vaccines even before the Chinese authorities completed their approval processes. The transactions were syphoned through an anonymous offshore company. As is the rule in Hungary under Viktor Orban's corrupt regime, all the documents were made top secret for decades. Even more outrageous, the cost of these vaccines has been three or four times higher than the Pfizer and Moderna vaccines. The thus-acquired vaccines have been forced on the population that has protested strenuously against such an authoritarian measure. Meanwhile, the European Union has done nothing. Brussels has continued to underwrite the Hungarian economy that would go bankrupt without the annual disbursement of 5.3 billion Euros.

The global impact of Chinese corruption has been devastating, especially for the economies of developing countries. Fighting and rooting out corrupt Beijing influence and designs internationally is key to economic developments across the globe. Pursuant to a 2018 report by the United Nations (UN), worldwide corruption is estimated to cost at least $2.6 trillion or 5% of the global GDP. Beyond the economic, financial, and cultural damage, pervasive corruption also destroys those countries' progress toward developing genuinely democratic institutions.

Therefore, decisive countering of Chinese corruption is essential. Beijing's strategy of also buying up corrupt governments and politicians in Africa, Central and South America, and South-East Asia should not stand because it will lead to a corrupt world ruled by the Chinese Communist Party and its Politburo.

As a clear confirmation of Chinese duplicity and an additional slap in the face of the international community and the WHO, on May 15, 2020, Liu Dengfeng, a supervisor with China's National Health Commission and essentially a low-level bureaucrat within the Chinese government, admitted that "the Chinese government issued an order on January 3rd to dispose of 'coronavirus samples' at unauthorized laboratories." As reported by Newsweek, Mr. Liu denied that the samples were terminated in order to conceal evidence. Rather, he claimed, it was done to comply with Chinese public health laws to "prevent risk to laboratory biological safety and prevent secondary disasters caused by unidentified pathogens." He also stated that the laboratories at issue were "unauthorized" to handle such samples. Yet, they did.

Of course, his lame excuses and explanations beg the question, why was the Chinese government so confused about the identity of the new pathogen? If the pathogen was "unidentified," how could government authorities ascertain that it was so dangerous it had to be destroyed immediately without conducting any further research? Finally, if this new pathogen posed such a biological safety risk that it had to be eliminated, why did China conceal both the existence and the destruction of the pathogen from the WHO until May 15, 2020, and lie about it incessantly?

According to a later study by the Harvard Medical School in early June 2020, satellite images showed "a dramatic increase" in the number of cars parked outside six major Wuhan hospitals in September 2019 with a peak in traffic in December 2019. "Individual hospitals have days of high relative volume in both fall and winter 2019. However, between September and October 2019, five of the six hospitals show their highest relative daily volume of the analyzed series", the case study opined.

In addition, researchers also saw increased internet traffic on search terms relating to COVID-19 like symptoms, such as coughing and diarrhea, on the Chinese search engine Baida. Dr. John Brownstein, the leader of the research team, told ABC News, "Clearly, there was some level of social disruption taking place well before what was previously identified as the start of the novel coronavirus pandemic."

Chinese manipulations concerning the origin of the coronavirus pandemic have continued unabated until today. The most recent WHO report on the origins of COVID-19 have been termed "outrageous" by WHO adviser Jamie Metzl because the Wuhan laboratory leak hypothesis was not seriously investigated. He stated, "What they said is that they were given the task of examining the zoonotic (animal) origin of the pandemic. So in the framing of the task, a conclusion was already implicit. And so that was why, according to them, they didn't have the mandate or the capacity or the skills or the team or the access to even investigate. And so you could not have a legitimate process without examining all of the hypotheses. They only examined some." He also added that China should not be rewarded for its cover-up, including the destruction of samples, the removal of access from databases, the imprisonment of journalists, and the placement of universal gag orders on Chinese scientists.

Obviously, Beijing cannot credibly investigate these questions. Continuing to lie ad infinitum is also not an option in the world of social media and high technology spying. While President Xi and his colleagues can follow Paul Joseph Goebbels' dictum of repeating a lie often enough to brand it as the truth, the Chinese Communist leadership fell into a classic trap. The bubble of the illusion of truth burst, and the leaders of the People's Republic were exposed as loathsome mini emperors without clothing. Although, as the saying goes, hope springs eternal. A reasonable person would not bet his money on President Xi and his colleagues to learn their lessons from the COVID-19 fiasco. It is more likely that they will continue to lie, bribe, obfuscate, and disseminate hateful propaganda in order to advance their final solution of ruling the world.

But the most damning evidence came from a resident of Wuhan by the name of Fang Fang who wrote a diary of the local coronavirus history. She published her diary in chronological increments on her blog between January 25 and March 24, 2020. Published on May 17, 2020, by the *Sunday Times*, she revealed that her brother, a professor of Huazhong University of Science and Technology, told her the virus was highly contagious and transferable among humans. She contrasted her brother's statement with the official propaganda that asserted the non-contagious character of the novel coronavirus as "Not contagious between people; it's controllable and preventable." Fang Fang wrote in great detail about the scramble for facemasks, food, and supplies, while hospitals all over the city of 11 million teetered on the brink of collapse.

Her February 13, 2020, entry described the chaotic conditions inside a local crematorium, illustrating the scenes with photographs taken by her friend and showing a "pile of mobile phones on the floor of a funeral home; the owners of those phones had already been reduced to ash." Other entries in Fang Fang's diary were full of horrific tales of desperate residents, ages 3 to 80, who were left alone amidst the ubiquitous chaos to fend for themselves. Even more significantly, she noted that her physician friends knew from the beginning that there was human-to-human transmission of the disease which they reported to their superiors without any noticeable results.

Vividly showing the real nature of the regime, a campaign was launched to destroy Fang Fang intellectually as well as physically. Accused of being a "Hanjian," a traitor to the Han Chinese, her life was threatened. Stoking the flames of racial hatred, Hu Xijin, editor in chief of the ultranationalist tabloid *Global Times*, wrote that the foreign publications of the diary "are not really in good taste."

Raising the stakes of Chinese intentions, *The Daily Wire* reported on May 8, 2021, that the U.S. government is in the possession of a document in which scientists in the Chinese military discuss the possible weaponization of the SARS coronavirus to win a third world war. According to Ryan Saavedra, the report's author, "The document, written by People's Liberation Army scientists and senior Chinese public health officials in 2015, was obtained by the U.S. State Department as it conducted an investigation into the origins of COVID-19." Quoting from *The Weekend Australian*, Mr. Saavedra asserts, "The paper [the Chinese document in question] describes SARS coronaviruses as heralding a 'new era of genetic weapons' and says they can be artificially manipulated into an emerging human-disease virus, weaponized and unleashed in a way never seen before."

A Roman saying coined by the poet Seneca comes to mind, "Veritas nunquam perit." The truth never perishes, even when it is killed from time to time. From the inception of Mao's Chinese Socialism, the Chinese Communist Party has forced the people to lie and simultaneously actively deny the truth. Another great European who lived between the 18th and 19th centuries is Klemens Wenzel Nepomuk Lothar, Prince of Metternich-Winneburg zu Beilstein. When analyzing the causes for the failure of the French King Louis Phillipe, who ruled between 1830 and 1848, Lothar said in volume 5 of his memoirs, "Condemned to hover between two realities, Monarchy and Republic, Louis Phillipe is in a vacuum, for a lie is a vacuum."

In the case of the People's Republic of China, this version of Chinese despotism was also founded on a lie—the lie that Maoism would bring about the perfect utopia in the form of heavenly peace and stability to the Chinese people and the rest of the world. Instead, what four generations of Chinese have gotten in reality is thus far indescribable sufferings, ubiquitous misery, devastating famines, and senseless political terror.

Such a despotic regime is extremely vulnerable and therefore cannot endure for long. Albeit, it outwardly appears to be strong and stable, but historically, no despotism based on total oppression has been able to maintain itself indefinitely by sheer force. By demonstrating ruthless power at home and abroad, the Chinese Communist Party only attempts to conceal its fear from being challenged decisively and by an even more determined force. The United States of America and the rest of the world should realize that although the military, economic, and financial strength of the People's Republic are facts, they lack the solid political foundation that democracy provides the United States of America and many other countries across the globe. For these reasons, the outcome of any future global confrontation would not favor a despotic People's Republic of China.

Finally, the People's Republic of China has become the world's largest creditor to corrupt and money-hungry political leaders. According to the International Forum for Right and Security (IFFRAS), its joint research with the Peterson Institute for International Economics, the Kiel Institute for the World Economy, and the Centre for Global Development Aid concluded that Beijing uses its financial might to "debt trap" poor underdeveloped countries. Accordingly, Chinese credit terms are one-sided, shamefully favoring Chinese lenders. Moreover, credit terms are declared top secret and cannot be made public. Finally, Chinese contracts use language that renders repayment of loans a priority, thus gaining the upper hand over those countries' finances as well as economic and foreign policies.

Alarming for Beijing however, these Chinese practices coupled with the Chinese/Wuhan Covid-19 virus coverup are turning into a highly damaging scandal for China. Its toxic politicization of COVID-19 and its blatantly racist expansionism have had extremely negative global ramifications. In this manner, President Xi Jinping's overreach by parroting the Chinese narrative has already created a burgeoning anti-Chinese wave of sentiment against the People's Republic of China. His "Chinese Exceptionalism" will surely globally stymie his imperialist design.

2

A Personal Perspective

HISTORICALLY, HUMANS HAVE been prone to succumb to lies when they have been surrounded by inimical political, economic, social, cultural, and moral conditions that make their minds vulnerable to pathological limitations on their abilities to differentiate between reality and illusion. Living under such antisocial and even psychopathic circumstances condemns the individual to lead an artificial existence in which the truth turns into falsehood and falsehood becomes reality. Experiencing the destructive effects of authoritarian unrealities on an entire nation and even half a continent in Europe in person, I decided from a very early age to resist and actively fight against every intentionally enforced treacherous mass distortion of reality.

I was born after the end of World War II when the 20th century tsar of the Soviet Union Josif Vissarionovich Dzhugashvili, also dubbed as Stalin, occupied most of Eastern and Central Europe and introduced his Soviet-style Communist dictatorship in those countries. Until the age of 10, I grew up in a city in middle-Hungary designated as the "Famous City" on account of its Middle Age resistance to the Ottoman occupation. Thus, the ethos of freedom and independence were deeply ingrained in the traditions of Kecskemet. Even the city's coat of arms depicts a salient goat who is ready to defend and attack at the same time. Its origin dates back to 1554. Going back to 1809, ,its motto of "neither the height nor the depth shall deter" was taken from the Apostle Paul's letter to the Romans (Romans 8:39).

Understandably, the military occupation and subsequent imposition of Communist dictatorship on Hungary shocked the entire nation. My hometown was not an exception. The newly installed Matyas Rakosi, dubbed "Little Stalin" by the Hungarians, brought about a bloody terror campaign against everybody, including loyal Communists. The State Defense Authority (Hungarian acronyms: AVH) united the responsibilities of the police, the prosecutor, and the judge in itself.

My father's as well as my mother's families were well known in the city. Prior to World War II, my paternal grandfather, a Jew by the name of Sandor Roth, owned the only slaughterhouse in the city and most of the apartment buildings along the main street. My maternal grandfather was born in the city of Kolozsvar, located in the eastern part of the Hungarian Kingdom called Transylvania which became a part of the new Romanian Kingdom after 1918. He was a devout Lutheran and belonged to a group of Transylvanian Hungarians called "Szekely."

When my mother started dating my father in 1941, my grandfather and one of his sons-in-law reported my father to the authorities as an anti-German Jew. As a physician, he was arrested, taken to forced "Work Service," and sent to the front in the Soviet Union as a medical doctor. Upon his return, he was remanded to a ghetto in the city and sent to the Mauthausen annihilation camp in Austria. My father did survive, albeit with a serious heart condition. Upon his return, he married my mother. Her precondition was that he must convert to the Lutheran faith before the wedding. He did and changed his family name from Roth to the ancient Hungarian name Radvanyi.

My father had to attend a medical school in Bologna, Italy, because the Hungarian government legislated that Jews could only attend universities in proportion to their ratio to the Hungarian population, so he was excluded from being able to apply to one of the medical schools in Hungary. The bill was passed in 1920, two years before Mussolini's black shirts marched into Rome and three years before Hitler's infamous speech in the Beer Hall Putsch in Munich. The Hungarian bill was called Numerus Clausus, the Latin equivalent of closed numbers. Since the falsification of history has become an extremely popular national sport from time immemorial in Hungary, the country's (and its citizens') shameful participation in the genocide of over 600,000 Jews is still shrouded in a fog of lies, obfuscations, and pseudo-realities.

In 1948, my father was named the chief physician of the gynecology department of both the county hospital as well as the medical center in the city. He was a well-liked physician with a golden heart. Clearly, I was brought up amidst the raging political terror in relative privilege. Having been isolated from the ubiquitous misery and taught in school that Communist Hungary was already an earthly paradise, I believed my teachers' lies. My parents, as everybody else, were afraid of talking with me about anything even remotely political. The aftermath of the 1956 Revolution changed my early life.

My epiphany came at the age of 10 when the new Hungarian government allowed my father to accept a medical position in Israel. We spent almost five years in a country in which the pioneering spirit of building a new state for the people who were persecuted for two millennia and only survived in increments when the holocaust was at its height. The sheer enthusiasm, self-sacrifice, and all-pervasive feeling of national unity was overwhelming and contagious.

In those years, I became an unadulterated devotee of democracy. I attended many campaign events with my Jewish friends. For me to hear that then-Prime Minister David Ben Gurion, also affectionately called the Father of Israel, was regularly called a cheat, a crook, a criminal, and even worse by the opposition was a real eye opener. To illustrate the depth of freedom, I would like to retell a widely circulating joke in Israel in the late 1950s.

It went like this—three Rabbis were sitting at the same table in a restaurant, sipping tea and chatting amicably together. The joke was that in Israel, everybody knew there wasn't three Rabbis who could sit in agreement around the same table in any restaurant in the entire country. Yet in spite of their quarrelsome disposition and strong disagreements about almost everything, no Israeli citizen supported anti-democratic views or advocated economic and social policies that were hostile to the teachings of the Torah, Talmud, and traditions of the Jewish nation. As their religion, Judaism was the key to the strength and advancement of their nation. Religious unity in turn created a strong sense of political confidence.

At the age of 15, we returned to Hungary. Crossing the border from Austria and entering Hungary proper was like descending from normalcy into a human cemetery full of living dead. To begin with, several border guard officers escorted my father, mother, sister, and me from the train to four separate rooms. I was first interrogated about hidden jewelry and dollars. Then the real questioning started. They asked me about the schools, friends, acquaintances, and my views about Hungary. My answers visibly surprised them. Based on the freedom of information that was prevalent in Israel, I provided them with a fairly extensive analysis of the international and local situations.

After two hours of incessant questioning, we were allowed to reboard the train and proceed to Budapest. The main train terminal, called the "Western" and designed by French architect Alexandre-Gustave Eifel, was dark and dreary. Driving through Pest and proceeding to Buda, the city appeared to be scantily lit. During the following days after meeting relatives and old acquaintances, I realized the people were lacking even a semblance of confidence, freedom, and hope for the future. I felt the entire country was infected with a distorted and suicidal herd mentality. Reading the Communist Party-controlled newspapers and watching the monotonous and amateurish news on television reinforced my opinion that Hungarians had become hostages of an unreal, cult-like world.

When I rejoined a high school as a sophomore, my fellow students and I were not merely taught. We were mostly indoctrinated. Mainly, we were told humanity is divided into three classes: the working class, the peasantry, and the intelligentsia. Being born into the third class is inherently evil because members of the intelligentsia have historically been hostile to the other two classes and thus guilty of all of the bad actions done by others in the past and those that might be committed in the present as well as in the future against them, unless the ruling Communist Party, in its ultimate wisdom and power, prevents such injustices. The slogan of equity over equality must determine the place of everyone in society.

The bourgeois notion of equality and dignity of all human beings was thought to be a false capitalist idea that had only fostered exploitation and oppression of the working class as well as the peasantry. Therefore, equality must be replaced with equity that allowed the Communist Party to treat Hungarians unequally based on the Marxist categories of political classes. Finally, discrimination in the job markets and admission to schools of higher education and in courts was not only justified but mandatory for achieving an ideally classless society.

Of course I rebelled. My rebellion resulted in getting kicked out of two different high schools. As a senior, I was called into the principal's office who confronted me with a simple question, "Do you want to graduate from high school?" When I answered his question in the affirmative, he gave me simple advice, "Then shut your mouth!" Having heeded his advice, I graduated from high school and applied to the School of Political and Legal Sciences at the elite Budapest University of Eotvos Lorand. I was initially rejected on political grounds, but because of the intervention of an influential friend of my father's, I was admitted with a special permit by the minister of justice.

My class was full of the children of Communist potentates, based on the Communist version of affirmative action. These so-called students did not earn their admission on the merit of their school accomplishments. They were children of Communist Party officials, workers, and peasants who fought for the author-itarian regime. Their admissions were justified by the loyalty of their parents and not by the children's abilities to compete fairly in the real world. In this artificially maintained political climate, "social connections" were more important than actual mental abilities. In reality, the "progressive" Communist regime guided by Marx's "Scientific Socialism" was a semi-feudal government with the Communists being the aristocracy and the masses being mere subjects of an appalling, class-based despotism.

In this totally false "paradise" in which both the rulers and the ruled lived in existential fear, the Communist cowards and fraudulent rulers had the monopoly of power. And they used their power ruthlessly. They enforced a world that was imaginary and unreal. Thus, Hungarians existed in a fake society in which everybody pretended to be satisfied, if not happy, with their artificial world. In reality, they were divided into loyalists, also known as antisocial psychopaths, and enemies, also known as normal people. Yet, the psychopaths ruled over the normal people.

Decades later, the brilliant late Hungarian comedian Geza Hofi mused in one of his politically charged monologues, "The setting on this stage depicts a closed psychiatric ward in a hospital that specializes on mentally ill patients. I am a patient in this institution. I closed it from the inside to prevent all those idiots living outside from coming in." In his admonition, he wanted to call attention to the destructive state of affairs in Hungary in which initially normal people could be fooled by politically and ideologically demented persons masquerading as sane and responsible public figures, lose their minds, and join the herd of useful idiots.

The apparent travesty of establishing an impossible world with the assistance of Soviet military occupation of Hungary was also in full display when I entered the workforce. Sent by the government to the prosecutorial office of my home town, I became a useful "screw" in the badly functioning machine of the authoritarian Communist government. Having labored for three years as a prosecutor, I escaped Hungary on a dreary Sunday, January 9, 1973, and went to the Federal Republic of Germany.

Amidst the obligatory sentencing to prison in absentia, I joined Radio Free Europe. My message to my former countrymen was a warning against the almighty immorality in the form of mental and material corruption. I told them that permanently living a lie is horrific and will only generate countless individual and national tragedies on a scale as of yet unimaginable to them and their offspring. As proof of my warnings, I would like to refer to the fact that even today Hungary is heading the list in the world in the number of suicides per 1,000 inhabitants. After spending four more years in a scientific institute in Munich, I was offered a job in Washington, D.C., with a research unit of the Library of Congress. As a new citizen, I was also detailed to the Reagan White House and the United States Supreme Court in quick succession.

I am deeply appreciative of being an American citizen and that my children and grandchildren can live in a free country. As far as my country of birth is concerned, it has still not recovered from the disease of the Soviet-invented Communist/Socialist nightmare. In my opinion, Hungary as a free and democratic country does not exist, and its present as well as its future is extremely dire. In reality, Hungary is beyond redemption.

The lesson I personally learned from my experiences is summarized brilliantly by Matthew 7:24-27, "Anyone who listens to my teaching and follows it is wise, like a person who builds a house on solid rock. Though the rain comes in torrents and the floodwaters rise and the winds beat against that house, it won't collapse because it is built on bedrock. But anyone who hears my teaching and doesn't obey it is foolish, like a person who builds a house on sand. When the rains and floods come and the winds beat against the house, it will collapse with a mighty crash."

Indeed, the Marxism-based Communist/Socialist regimes were founded on a bed of sand consisting of lies and distorted realities. They were fraudulent because they demonstratively mocked the history and experience of humanity. Moreover, they abused reality and the powers they acquired deceitfully. Finally, the immorality of Communism/Socialism robbed both the individual and society of their dignity because its followers turned the natural notions of good and evil on their heads. Having declared normalcy unnatural and their pathological idiocy normal, they dared the sane people to demonstrate that reality could override unreality. This double standard and the ruthlessly enforced distinction between "them" and "us" fueled chaos and anarchy that rendered the despotic rulers' power overreach absolutely untenable for their subjects.

In addition, I have also learned that a country can only be liked when the individual can call it his or her home. When I returned to Hungary following a long absence, I realized that my home is in the United States of America and not in my country of birth. Indeed, the bedrock upon which the United States of America was built is its traditional and timeless Judeo-Christian ethos and not the idiotic notions of Cancel Culture, Identity

Politics, Critical Race Theory, big lies about White racism, and systematic and institutionalized racism.

The reality of America's goodness has been under terrorist attack, both pseudo-intellectually as well as violently, by a minority whose only objective has been to seize power and wealth from the majority. Among the countless terrorist attempts to annihilate Judeo-Christian governance which is the most dangerous is a city ordinance by Kansas City Mayor Quinton Lucas, a Democrat, who ordered pastors to turn over the names, addresses, and phone numbers of anyone who enters church houses. The ordinance reads, "Religious gatherings, including but not limited to, weddings, funerals, memorial services, and wakes, of ten persons inside or ten percent of building occupancy (whichever number is greater) and fifty people may resume, provided social distancing is maintained and event organizers maintain a record of attendees."

All of this, of course, with the humanitarian intention to save lives amidst the COVID-19 pandemic. Thus, under the guise of fighting the spread of the coronavirus, Mayor Lucas feels entitled to violate the constitutional principle of separation of state and church and impose measures previously employed by despotic regimes elsewhere, but not in the United States of America—until now.

Even more disconcerting, an increasing number of public schools and teachers are making their own attempts to punish students for writing and talking about God. Their justification is as surreal as a lie. They claim that writing about God in school could violate the first amendment in the classroom. To add outrageous insult to unconstitutional injury, many principals and teachers encourage other students to openly mock religious students' belief in God which creates a hostile school environment across the nation. This hostile environment is definitely exacerbated by the same teachers' enthusiastic promotion of Critical Race Theory which is vulgar Marxism at its worst. Former Attorney General Bill Barr is convinced that this anti-religious agenda is unconstitutional.

To wit, Democrat governors and mayors across the land have been abusing their rights under the pandemic to radically transform the country to their pathological and fraudulent image. Hawk Newsome, who chairs Black Lives Matter of Greater New York, argues that because violence and rioting have appeared to be getting the point across more effectively, those actions have been justifiable. This has resulted in the belief that it is proper in a democracy for a small and unreasonably disgruntled small minority to tell the overwhelming majority how to live and what to think.

This "the end justifies the means" mentality is self-obsessed, arrogant, and devoid of any rational tolerance or empathy. Essentially, Mr. Newsome, in his idiotic self-righteousness, has declared that the mob and the thugs have the right to illegally rule over the majority. Accordingly, he has expressed his intention to "shove legislation down people's throats." Overpowered by raw emotion that has clearly befogged his limited intellect, he intoned thus, "If this country doesn't give us what we want then we will burn down the system and replace it." What Mr. Newsome and his comrades-in-arms really want is the absolute power of a despotic minority. Then drunk with this power, they will destroy everything, including themselves, because they do not have the faintest idea of what the replacement should be or how to govern at all.

More specifically, the Los Angeles chapter of Black Lives Matter has demanded the resignation of County District Attorney Jackie Lacey an African American and card-carrying radical liberal, for failing to prosecute more police officers who were involved in fatal shootings during her tenure in office. Melina Abdullah, one of the co-founders of the city's Black Lives Matter chapter, castigated District Attorney Lacey for not taking more cases to court. Her complaint is, of course, outrageous. On the one hand, she is not even superficially acquainted with those cases. On the other hand, she was neither elected or appointed to the position Ms. Lacey has occupied. For Ms. Abdullah, talking more than listening, playing the victim, treating others who disagree with her disparagingly, criticizing everybody without factual basis, and employing lies to support her false narratives are justified in the name of political correctness paired with racial wrath.

The case of Chanelle Helm is even more extreme. This co-founder of Black Lives Matter has demanded that White folks should transfer all of their properties to the descendants of slaves, allegedly in the name of social justice. "White people, if you don't have any descendants, will your property to a black or brown family. Preferably one that lives in generational poverty." In her article published on August 17, 2017, she laid out 10 requests to "White People."

Among these gems are some that are more idiotic than the rest. For example, number seven states, "White people, especially white women (because this is yaw specialty—Nosey Jenny and Meddling Kathy), get a racist fired. Yaw know what the fuck they are saying. You are complicit when you ignore them. Get your boss fired because they racist too." Furthermore, "Backing up No. 7, this should be easy but all the sheetless Klan, Nazi's and other lil' dick-white men will be all returning to work. Get their ass fired. Call the police even: they look suspicious." Then the following, "OK, backing up No. 8, if any white person at your work, or as you enter in spaces and you overhear a white person praising the action of yesterday, first, get a pic. Get their name and more info. Hell, find out where they work—Get Them Fired. But certainly address them, and, if you need to, you got hands: use them." In addition, "Commit to two things: Fighting white supremacy where and how you can (this doesn't mean taking up knitting, unless you're making scarves for black and brown kids in need) and funding black and brown people and their work."

A fine example of neo-racist sentiments can also be found in the writings of another co-founder of the Black Lives Matter movement. Ms. Yusra Khogali, a Sudanese refugee and self-professed proud Marxist, believes that White people are "subhuman" and should be "wiped out." To demonstrate her African-American, Muslim, and Marxist compassion in a single prayer in one of her tweets, now mercifully deleted, she begged Allah to give her the strength not to "kill white people." According to *The National Pulse*, the deleted tweet said the following verbatim, "Plz Allah give me the strength to not cuss/kill these men and white folks out here today: Plz plz plz."

Predictably, her tweets have been in line with umpteenth prayers, statements, and utterances of Muslim politicians and religious scholars as well as the faithful who have quoted the Prophet Mohammad's words that Judgment Day for faithful Muslims will not come before the Muslims fight the Jews, and the Jews will hide behind the rocks and the trees, but the rocks and the trees will say, "Oh Muslim, oh servant of Allah, there is a Jew behind me, come and kill him—except for the gharqad tree, which is one of the trees of the Jews." Clearly, this good-for-nothing fake refugee has simply replaced Jews for Whites. And as behooves a genuine Marxist, compassionate and faithful follower of Islam (erroneously dubbed religion of peace), and an expert in medical sciences without any real education, she opines that White people possess "recessive genetic defects" and should be "wiped out."

Moreover, on her Facebook page, she asserts that "whiteness is not humxness" and "white skin is sub-humxn." For her insightful comments like these, she received a Canadian government-sanctioned "Young Women in Leadership Award" in 2018. O Canada! Indeed! How proud you could be of your sage government! Obviously, in light of such a serious case of psychological derangement, some questions arise ... Why did she come to the United States of America in the first place? Who let her in? Why doesn't she leave and go back to Sudan? Why has she not been arrested for a long list of crimes? Why has she not been examined by a qualified psychiatrist? And finally, why has she not already been remanded to a closed mental institution as a cautionary and preemptive measure?

In their violent and hate-filled tribalism, these pathological psychopaths subscribe to the Latin dictum, "Qui perde, peche." Those who lose are guilty too because they are convinced they will win and the majority will lose. A dearth of boundaries in decency invites lawlessness. The abandonment of reality and the rule of law has historically been the first step on the path of national suicide. For this reason alone, when the Biden administration pretends to function as a normal government while taking away the tools to maintain law and order from the competent agencies of the government, it makes a mockery out of the entire legal system of the United States of America.

Similarly, the Black Lives Matter radical and lawless organization and its adherents have failed to understand from the start that their sole focus on violence, mayhem, and destruction has made them lose sight of what they have earned and have deserved. Just rampaging and pillaging to achieve dubious political goals is unacceptable in a society governed by the rule of law. For these reasons, these organizations have nothing to do with the civil rights movement led by Martin Luther King in the 1960s. On the contrary, they are the political and ideological opposites of the color-blind American liberalism.

Another gaslighting aspect of these extremists' and out-of-bound idiots' demands has been that in education, Blacks should not be required to meet the same standards demanded from White, Asian, and Hispanic students. According to this self-defeating ultimatum, Blacks admit they are not as smart as others, and therefore in the name of social justice, they should be positively discriminated against. Advocating the dumbing down of education, such as denouncing mathematics as proof of White supremacy, is tantamount to relegating the United States of America to a second grade status in international science. Employing reverse racism in the age of a new technological revolution with the dawn of the artificial intelligence (AI) era demonstrates that Blacks in their intellectual misery cannot even grasp the elementary currents in today's world. The utter idiocy of such a condition is too obvious to further elaborate on.

In a normal society, there is agreement over the dictum that mental patients cannot run the asylum. For this reason alone, this idiocy of a miniscule minority of the Black community must be decisively stopped right now. The Black Lives Matter, Antifa, and like-minded extremist mobs are like cancers growing in a healthy body. If these malignant and pseudo-intellectual cancers are allowed to metastasize, the United States of America and the rest of the Free World will face a catastrophic future.

Woefully, Americans live in a time when most normal people have stopped thinking for themselves in order to not offend the feelings and narratives of the idiots. For this reason, the United States of America is paralyzed with fear because of those idiots who have declared an all-out war on all sane persons, namely, the vast majority of the American population. The Black mobs fraudulent ideologies, such as the absolutely fallacious narrative of the "1619 Project," is the product of the same psychopathic opportunists who hate everybody, including themselves, because they know that they robbed themselves of credibility as well as integrity for the sake of power and money.

While history's great minds have served humanity by their intellects, these Black psychopathic opportunists are doing so exclusively through their negative and destructive emotions. Their inability to comprehend reality and the catastrophic consequences of their ruinous actions will surely result in their ultimate destruction of any spiritual connection with the people they falsely claim to represent.

Yet, the Biden administration just announced that the government is ready to offer grants to teach children the 1619 Project's inherently hateful and treacherous neo- racist narrative. Listed in the Federal Register, the grant program for all K-12 schools promotes the fallacious assertions of Ibram X. Kendi, a

Black so-called professor and pioneer in Critical Race Theory. The gist of his theory is that White people as a race are guilty of perpetuating systematic racism, regardless of their verbal communications and actions. The cure for his false narrative is uncompromising and all-out reverse discrimination in order to totally destroy White supremacist institutions.

For the mentally challenged Biden administration and its psychopathic fellow travelers in the media that are hell-bent to deny objective information to the American public, the fact that Ivy League professors uniformly have stated that the 1619 Project is bogus does not appear to matter. What matters for them is showing that slavery has been the most important defining feature of American history. Accordingly, the year 1619, the year when the first slaves arrived in the Colonies, marked the "true founding" of America. Even more outrageously, the 1619 Project claims the American Revolution was exclusively driven by the desire to perpetuate slavery in the Colonies.

However, most disconcertingly, this psychopathic ideology, as the other like-minded Black ideologies, temporarily creates a psychopathic state of mind in otherwise normal individuals. As it happened in Communist Hungary and throughout the Soviet Empire, nobody really believed in Marxism, Communism, or Socialism, but they served it out of fear for they would otherwise be labeled enemies of the people. And herein lies the absolute immorality of these two inherently false narratives. According to both, immorality is good, while morality is evil. With time, as in Hungary as well as in the former Soviet Empire, normal individuals with few exceptions will become intellectually infected with the psychopathic garbage forced upon them by the criminal mob. The Judeo-Christian morality of kindness, tolerance, and empathy will be replaced by hatred, vicious jealousy, and total mayhem.

Clearly, it will be a gross dereliction of duty for the overwhelming majority to allow these immoral and lawless criminals and domestic terrorists to destroy America and the present as well as the future of successive generations with it. The harm they have already inflicted on domestic tranquility and the international positions of the United States of America is grave. It has reinforced a false narrative about American society as a heartless and hypocritical community. As a result, there has been ubiquitous instability and major conflicts across the globe.

Globally, there are two irreconcilable forms of government in the world—the democratic and the authoritarian. They are irreconcilable because these two forms of government cannot be merged into one by superficial concessions or unscrupulous compromises. The forced reconciliation of these two forms of government within a single country or beyond has already created umpteenth monster governments worldwide. As the shameful history of the Soviet Union and Hitler's Germany attests to, a government born of a utopian idea and conceived out of a heap of lies will always be doomed to catastrophic failure.

These two regimes' reigns were a cavalcade of terror and fear that horrifically lit the world on fire. A power that pretends to be democratic when it is authoritarian in reality and a government that pretends to represent the majority when it is not becomes corrupt and despotic necessarily. The inevitable outcome of such power is always total political and moral collapse. Black Lives Matter, Antifa, Critical Race Theory, and similar nonsensical Black inventions must be decisively rejected with great determination. Simultaneously, American politics must return to the Founding Fathers' core and humanistic principles and values.

Americans cannot find patriots more committed to the ideals of democracy and freedom than the Founding Fathers and most of the presidents who succeeded George Washington. Their adherence to equality, the rule of law, and the importance of perfecting democracy has been unquestionable. For them, democracy has meant equality and freedom for all. Slavery was a temporary aberration that has been rectified long ago. Blacks as well as other minorities have been guaranteed all the rights and tools to become constructive members of society.

Therefore, the rallying cries about "White supremacy" and "systematic and institutionalized racism" are great lies. What should be addressed here in all seriousness is the question about why some of them feel that things are going badly for their communities. If there is room for improvement in their political, economic, and educational developments, peaceful measures should be taken to rectify any shortcomings. However, these measures must be taken within the framework of the rule of law. Under no circumstances should additional emergency legislation be adapted. This extremist and terroristic minority should not be allowed to move American democracy toward an avalanche of tyrannical legislation.

Growing up, I learned that truth, honesty, trust, and kindness are irreplaceable. When they have been lost, they are mostly irretrievable. The alarm bells have been ringing for a while for the entire political, economic, and cultural spectrum because every American is responsible for the present and the future of his or her country. For the last five or six years, politicians and the media have lied, cheated, and covered up. They have based their behavior on their egotistical political and economic gains.

Accordingly, they have been busy molding America and the world to accommodate their pseudo-realities to the actual events in the real world. To accomplish their nefarious goals, they have often embraced policies they then betray by cynically performing shameful U-turns. For tactical reasons, they have embraced individuals and groups that they drop at the next available opportunity. They have abandoned the voters who have elected them and followed policies inimical to their voters' interests.

The United States of America is facing crucial domestic and foreign challenges that cannot be approached without a national consensus about the core values and a common language. The idiocy of public discourse that has held Americans hostage for the last five or six years must be terminated. The United States of

America needs a new comprehensive understanding of itself. For that, Americans need an honest and kind national conversation. Only after a thorough re-examination of who we are and what is most important for us can we heal our fractured society at home and be respected again abroad in a fragmented world.

3

The Destructive Orgy of the Anti-American Idiots

FOR ME PERSONALLY, the most important lesson of the last three decades in the United States of America has been the steadily deepening disaffection. During this period of time, too many Americans have had the unsettling feeling that their country is not living up to its ideals, and for this reason, they have been the victims of extremist single-issue groups and movements demanding impunity for their illegally destructive actions.

Woefully, since the early 1960s, the majority of Americans have elected to appease these violent minorities instead of confronting them. The result has been as expected—presently, these minorities are working tirelessly to destroy the United States of America and its republican form of government. Three decades later during the 1990s and on and with the colossal rise of illegal immigration, the same extremist groups and movements have declared that Blacks as well as first- and second-generation illegal immigrants are justified to complain about their unequal treatment regarding freedom and equality within American society. Sensing a political opening, the Democrat Party has jumped on the anti-assimilation bandwagon, declaring all forms of resistance to federal, state, and local governments fully justified and legitimate.

Assimilation is out and the glorification of multiculturalism has become a central issue in what has been in reality a much broader debate about national identity as well as the founding principles of the United States of America. Gradually, the unthinkable has happened. Instead of assimilating into the American way of life, Black and other minority youths have repeatedly erupted with high crime rates, frequent violent clashes with the authorities, the ritual burning of cars, looting businesses indiscriminately, and demanding impunity from well-deserved punishments. In this manner, they have forced America to carry the weight of its early history in its view of itself. Indeed, by having invoked the past in the form of slavery, they have called for totally eradicating the past and replacing it with a quasi-Marxist utopian future.

More plainly, these assorted minority groups and movements have always wanted to turn democracy into a dictatorship of minorities and a despotism of the mob. Though this opposition could not defeat the Union, it has represented a continuing source of instability and fear as different ideological variations metastasized into more violent actions across these political spectrums. The majority's refusal to face reality, in turn, has created an enormous civil disarray and a wave of individual catastrophes.

As Zoltan Kodaly, the world-renowned Hungarian composer, remarked, "Mankind cannot afford the luxury of idiocy." Clearly, the overwhelming majority of Americans sense they are living through a deep existential crisis of their cherished democracy. As Franz Kafka noted, "One idiot is one idiot. Two idiots are two idiots. Ten thousand idiots are a political party." More generally, when idiots are allowed to rewrite or even erase history instead of facing it, the truth will always be threatened or lost entirely.

In the two-party context of American politics, the misleadingly labeled progressives, also hypocritically called liberals, in their crude arrogance and deep-seated immorality, have cared more about building up their fake moral superiority infused with their utopian belief in authoritarian social engineering than about the unity of the nation and the equality of every individual.

On the other side of the political equation, the so-called traditionalists, also called conservatives, have flocked hesitatingly around the constitutional meaning of liberty, universal justice, and inherent political, economic, and social as well as moral equality. Yet lacking the desire to be unified, the traditionalists/conservatives have existed in continual disarray as contending individuals battled for leadership of an amorphous and multifactional Republican Party. Given the refusal of the majority of Black youth and illegal immigrants to integrate into American society because of large cultural differences together with the rejection of "White" values, the vacuum within the multiethnic and multiracial nation has widened exponentially.

In the liberal/progressive camp, the rallying cry has been revolution, meaning the complete destruction, deceitfully defined by them as "fundamental transformation," of the constitutional Republic. This assembly of sectarian revolutionaries have had no reservations about such a scorched-earth strategy as they have been blinded by their desire to create an out-of-this-world utopia exclusively for themselves. To add more surreality to their inherent idiocy, they have embarked on automatically labeling any opposition to their hyperbolic designs as racist, misogynistic, homophobic, immoral, and inhuman or, as Hillary Clinton so disparagingly stated during her deservedly unsuccessful presidential campaign in 2016, a "basket of deplorables."

The traditionalists/conservatives have complained that American democracy has not been working well because it has been undermined by the Democrat Party and the media. They have been repelled by most of the changes, claiming the overwhelming majority of the American people have been misled by the constant barrage of indoctrination, profound lies, and misrepresentations. However, the mainstream of the traditionalists/conservatives have been badly divided and have remained either on the fence or partially unsure of where they stand in a permanently changing world. Generally, they have been for change but through predominantly ill-defined or even ambiguous reforms.

Predictably, all of these zero-sum pursuits of ubiquitous change have only led to the over politicization of American politics as well as the emergence of multiple anarchist interest groups and extremist political movements. The most consequential result of these developments has been the partial or even total abandonment of fact-based objectivity and rationalism on both sides of the political spectrum. Even more confusing, the traditional meaning of words has been challenged by pseudo-academics as well as people with inferior intellect or no intellect at all, contributing mightily to the fearful terror of liberty of thought and freedom of speech.

Such a spiritual terrorism under the guise of "political correctness" recalls the Stalinist regime in the 1930s, 1940s, and 1950s in the Soviet Union where an "infallible" dictator was licensed to commit the most heinous crimes in order to bring about "universal happiness." In the lying history of the so-called "cancel culture," a self-victimized minority has undertaken to rob the past while trying to steal its heroes' achievements and services to the American nation and to the world for themselves. Likewise, with the guilty assistance of blatant lies and outlandish slanders, people who have dared to cast truth in the faces of these "neo-racist warriors" have been maligned and viciously persecuted by written and electronic media, especially social media.

Disparaging the past, gaslighting the present, and paying treacherous homage to a paradise-like utopian future have become routine actions by liberal/progressive circles these days. Consequently, the assiduous accumulation of irrational onslaughts on American and global cultures as the products of

"White supremacy" as well as "systematic and institutionalized White racism" has been utilized mostly by the Black minority (a mere 13.4% of the population) to denigrate and "cancel" history and universal culture through the great works of world literature imbued with humanism for mankind, especially for the less fortunate. Calling the concepts of nation and the resulting patriotism "myths" and praising "world citizenship" to high heavens, as Democrat candidate Barack Obama grandiloquently did in 2008 in Berlin to the ubiquitous amazement and ridicule of most Europeans as well as the rest of the world, has been designed to eliminate the foundations of democracy and individual freedom.

Regrettably, former-President Barack Obama and his wife have not stopped poisoning the well of fragmentation with their slanderous private and public statements. Paying tribute to George Floyd, the former president said, "But if we can turn words into actions and action into meaningful reform, we will, in the words of James Baldwin, 'cease fleeing from reality and begin to change it.'" To up the ante of his intellectual poverty, the former president appeared to mock White American parents on the Anderson Cooper Show on CNN for "stoking fear and resentment" against the curriculum that contains the Critical Race Theory (CRT).

Confusing understanding with ignorance, this hapless pseudo-intellectual erroneously argued that CRT is a harmless reality that is "fully reconciled with our history." As always, rich in empty and even stupid rhetoric but devoid of any intelligence, President

Obama cannot comprehend that he and his fellow travelers have been fleeing from reality for decades. Furthermore, if reality is a collection of facts, is he calling to change reality and the facts? Clearly, President Obama has not changed as he has gotten older. He continues to utilize the same discombobulated mind and the same deceptively comforting but meaningless idiocy.

Knowing full well that no stable present and viable future can be created on the rejection and even perpetual hatred of the past because hatred of the past ultimately leads to hatred of the history of mankind which in turn would culminate in hatred of one's fellow citizens and one's country, their final solution is total destruction of everything that stands in their way for absolute power and unbridled control of all financial and economic resources of the United States of America as well as the whole world.

Indeed, the overwhelming majority of Americans have mostly ignored the stealthily progressing poisonous attempts of the liberal/progressive movement to build an absolutely perfect society for themselves to the detriment of the constitutional Republic. Having classified this initially tiny minority as crazy loons existing on the fringes of society, Americans have thought that this minority's ideas were innocuous dreams that could never materialize in the real world. What has been overlooked was the history of similar utopian movements across the globe.

As a rule, the weirder the utopia has become, the more desperately the actions of its practitioners have progressed toward inhuman bestiality. Stripped of its token humanitarianism and demagogic social justice theory as well as perfect equality facades, Mussolini's Fascism, Hitler's National Socialism, and Lenin's as well as Stalin's Communism have all come to evil ends in their practitioners' hands. While Fascism and National Socialism were short-term catastrophes, Communism, or what became of it in Russia and then in the Soviet Union, lasted for more than seven decades before collapsing into the abyss of its incompetence, self-induced lies, unrealities, and irrational terror.

To wit, what the majority of Americans still have not grasped is the absolute incompatibility of and yawning chasm between false doctrinaire ideology and truthful authenticity. The difference between these two irreconcilable viewpoints is the degree of determination between the attackers, the liberal/progressives, and the defenders, the traditionalists/conservatives. The former are driven by their conviction that they are living in an unjust society in which they are the victims of the majority that oppresses them illegally, while the latter believe that the past and present are both on their side because both reinforce the rightness of the existing order. Again, although the past and present are used to condemn on one hand and justify on the other, the real issue here is this death confrontation for the future of the United States of America.

To best illustrate the vainglorious obsession, narrow-mindedness, and even intellectual stupidity of the traditionalists/conservatives, we should hark back to Senator Mitt Romney's craziest statements and actions. The former governor and Republican nominee for president declared during his 2012 campaign, "There are 47% of the people who will vote for the president [meaning sitting president Barack Obama] no matter what. All right, there are 47% who are with him, who are dependent upon government, (sic) who believe that they are victims, who believe the government has a responsibility to care for them, who believe that they are entitled to health care, to food, to housing, to you name it. […] My job is not to worry about those people. I'll never convince them they should take personal responsibility and care for their lives."

Really, Mitt? Your responsibility as the standard bearer of the Republican Party only extended to the rest of the population? Unfortunately, Mitt Romney's idiocy has not ended there. At a campaign event close to the elections on October 16, 2012, he said, "As President, I will create 12 million new jobs." Forty-five minutes later, he opined thus, "Government doesn't create jobs. Government doesn't create jobs."

During the dual impeachments of President Trump, Mitt Romney was again in his most idiotic best by voting for conviction at the first impeachment trial on the first article of abuse of power. His justification was a testament to his confused mind. He claimed to the Atlantic's McKay Coppins on February 5, 2020, that he was guided by his father's favorite verse of Mormon scripture, "Search diligently, pray always, and be believing, and all things shall work together for your good." As a caveat he added, "I don't pretend that God told me what to do."

Really, Mitt? The people of Utah did not elect God. Unfortunately, they elected you. Your actions as a senator are your responsibilities alone. After the second unsuccessful impeachment trial where Mitt Romney again voted to convict on article one as the lone Republican, he issued a lengthy statement in which he declared that President Trump was guilty as charged by the Democrat majority in the House of Representatives. As always, his statement, better called a weak justification, was replete with factual errors and subjective emotions.

On the House side of Congress, the Republican Party had Liz Cheney of Wyoming in a leadership position. She's the oldest daughter of former Vice President Dick Cheney. Cheney, who chaired the House Republican Conference, said about her vote to impeach President Trump for the events on January 6, 2012, "This is a vote of conscience. It's one where there are different views in our conference. But our nation is facing an unprecedented, since the Civil War, constitutional crisis. That's what we need to be focused on."

Liz Cheney was wrong. What she should have been focusing on is that both impeachments were lacking any constitutional grounds. Moreover, she should have looked into the history of both impeachments, the unconstitutional resistance, the relentlessly hateful propaganda campaign of the Democrat Party machine, and almost the entire media being against everything that President Trump and the Republican Party tried to accomplish between 2017 and 2021. Classically, she got lost wandering aimlessly among the trees without paying attention to the forest. In spite of all her shortcomings, she maintained her leadership position until May 12, 2021.

Before losing her position, Cheney appeared on the Neil Cavuto Show on April 14, 2021, where she told her host that if Donald Trump were the 2024 nominee, she would not support him. Finally, as a parting shot, she said, "My re-election will be a referendum on the Republican Party." No, Ms. Cheney! Your re-election will be a referendum by the good people of Wyoming about you, your performance, and the nature of your service to them. Hopefully, the majority of voters will rise to the challenge and vote according to their objective judgment. If this is the case, the outcome will be unquestionably certain.

Then there is the former Republican Speaker of the House of Representatives John Boehner. Having been awakened from his long alcohol-induced slumber to market his book, he gave a kiss-and-tell interview to *Politico*. Showing why he should not have served as a speaker, John Boehner pontificated thus, "We've got some of the smartest people in America who serve in the Congress, and we've got some of the dumbest. We've some of the nicest people you'd ever want to meet, and some that are Nazis. Congress is nothing more than a slice of America."

Asked about Congressman Jim Jordan, the always "gentleman" former speaker said, "F-k Jordan. F-k Chavez. They are both a-holes." In another like-minded interview with CBS on April 14, 2021, "mild-mannered" John Boehner called Texas Senator Ted Cruz a "jerk." Moreover, calling all of his former colleagues "morons" and "terrorists" in order to sell a book about himself while betraying his entire political career is a personal tragedy and a national disgrace.

His opinion of Fox News host Sean Hannity was uttered in the same "soft and gentlemanly" manner. He told *Politico* that he allegedly had a conversation with Hannity sometime in 2015. During that alleged conversation, he called Hannity "nuts." Proving that Boehner is exclusively about Boehner, he added, "We had a really blunt conversation. Things were better for a few months, and then it got back to being the same-old, same-old because I wasn't going to be a right-wing idiot." No, John. You are right. You are not a right-wing idiot. You are an idiot without any adjective. Period.

Another example of the traditionalists/conservatives' confusion from the Executive Branch is FBI Director Chris Wray's statement in which he told lawmakers that Antifa is an ideology and not an organization. Having faced a barrage of criticism and ridicule, he later explained that Antifa is a "real thing" and that the FBI has undertaken "any number of properly predicated investigations into what we would describe as violent anarchist extremists," including into individuals who have identified with Antifa. Yet, he reiterated his previous statement and again claimed, "It's [meaning Antifa] not a group or an organization. It's a movement or an ideology."

Proving how contagious a single stupid statement can be, Joe Biden stated during the first presidential debate on September 29, 2020, "His [meaning then President Trump] own FBI Director said [...] Antifa is an idea, not an organization." In reality, Antifa is an organization with a nihilist ideology. As such, they are anarchistic, extremely violent, and evil. They justify their existence and violent lawlessness by claiming to be the legitimate successors of the European anti-Fascist and anti-Nazi movements of the 1920s and 1930s. Actually, they are liars and manipulators. They submerge their destructive ideology under the deceptive and slanderous myth that the United States of America is a combination of Mussolini and Hitler's Fascism/National Socialism. Thus, instead of Antifa being an "idea", as FBI Director Chris Wray stupidly claimed, it is a disciplined and ruthlessly violent Sturmtruppe of the liberal/progressive crowd with an evil ideology.

To bolster this fallacious description of Antifa, so-called scholars, artists, and communist activists have been pushing the fantastic narrative for decades that the movement was born out of the righteous sense of injustice perpetrated by the White majority against the pure-in-heart minorities, especially the Black as well as the Hispanic communities. As the incorrigible pseudo-intellectual *Time Magazine* opined on November 18, 2018, in a piece headlined "What the Artist Behind a Comics-Style History of

Anti-Fascist Resistance Thinks You Should Know About Antifa"
and written by Lily Rothman, the allegedly best expert on this
movement, Gord Hill was interviewed.

According to this incompetent expert on Fascism and Antifa,
the essence of the movement is its "emphasis on physical and
ideological confrontation against fascist movements." Linking
Mussolini's Fascism and the Anti-Fascist Action in England in
the 1980s with the present political conditions in the United
States of America, he states that Antifa's violence "dwarfs" Islamic
terrorist attacks and the mayhem committed by "far-right
extremists." Remarkably, the exact same false discourse schemes
are repeated by Wikipedia and other unwholesomely distributed
publications.

In reality, there is little objective knowledge about Antifa in
the United States of America and beyond. To start with, Antifa's
righteous claim that it is "anti-Fascist" suggests that everyone who
opposes them are by definition "Fascists." Thus, former President
Trump's description of Antifa as a terrorist organization automatically renders the former a Fascist and his administration a
Fascist government. Similarly, the youth protest movements in
the 1980s in Western Europe that violently fought everything
from environmental pollution to capitalism were characterized
by base manipulation of ulterior emotions, physical mayhem,
and extreme dystopia. In the United States of America, the same
angry and privileged European youth with their pseudo-social

justice warriors mentality showed up in Seattle in 1999 during the protests against the World Trade Organization.

The pseudo-intellectual insincerity and racially motivated manipulation of people over their vulnerabilities has long resulted in Antifa's selective outrage. Fellow pseudo-intellectuals in academia whose careers depend on peer recognition have become accomplices in blocking real talent and in the process of dumbing down American youth, presently starting in kindergarten. Thus, Antifa and its fellow travelers with their reverse (im)morality, which holds evil as the most valuable and goodness based on kindness as evil, are trapped in a hell of their own making. Moreover, lacking real critical thinking, their slogans and actions are false and invalid. As throughout human history when even the most brilliant alchemists could not produce gold from excrement, so an ideologically fallacious pseudo-philosophy is totally incapable of turning falsehoods into convincing reality.

As an another slap in the face of truth and reality, the Democrat Party as well as the overwhelming majority of the ideologically poisonous media have declared in unison that Antifa is a "largely peaceful" collection of young people who only voice and attempt to pursue legitimate democratic aspirations toward social justice, racial equality, and recognition of multiculturalism. In truth, the Democrat Party uses Antifa and likeminded organizations as proxies in their political war for absolute dictatorial power. Clearly, Antifa is a lawless organization whose members find personal and collective gratification in cruelty and destruction. Therefore, Americans, including members of the Democrat Party and all of the media, must reject the destructive ideology as well as the violent mass evil practiced by this organization.

Likewise, Black Lives Matter has manifested itself throughout its short existence as an organization with an extremely destructive modus operandi and genuinely neo- racist ideology. Again, the chasm between the organization's publicly advertised lofty goals and reality has been striking, yet the chasm between the illusions the organization has generated, mostly among Blacks, is even more catastrophic.

Having racked in around $90 million since its creation in 2012, according to the Black Lives Matter Global Network Foundation, Black Lives Matter only activates itself when a White policeman tries to restrain a Black person. For example in the case of George Floyd, who was allegedly in the process of turning his life around, paid for beer and cigarettes with a forged $20 bill while being high on lethal drugs, and when caught red handed, Floyd doggedly resisted arrest. Comparable acts, when White and non-Black people were violently attacked by Black teenagers and adults, the biased media defined them as "accidents."

Fittingly, the organization's heroes are Michael Brown, Jr., of St. Louis and George Floyd of Minneapolis. Recently, the 20-year-old Daunte Wright of Brooklyn Center, Minneapolis, has joined the list of these two hardened criminals who have been made fake innocent victims and the inglorious heroes of

Antifa, Black Lives Matter, and other anarchist groups and organizations. The common denominator is their extensive criminal past and violent refusal to follow the lawful commands of the police.

As President Biden stated in his demented stupidity, "Dr. King's assassination did not have the worldwide impact that George Floyd's death did." This unconditional belief in lies has been the real ideology of the Democrat Party, Black Lives Matter, and Antifa. Such an offense against the truth could only lead to the enforced terror of mindless conformity within the struggling majority of Blacks which only prevents them from properly assimilating into the larger American nation.

Michael Brown has been portrayed as a gentle giant full of goodness and love in his heart for every human being, according to the lying media's recent modus operandi. Actually, he has accumulated a long criminal record during his short life. On his crime sheet, assaults, robberies, and smaller misdemeanors show a young Black man with an attitude of entitlement because of belonging to a victimized minority. While eulogized as an ordinary young boy bound for college, he was scheduled to appear at court the September following his death for burglary, armed criminal mischief, and assault with the intent to do great bodily harm. Before his death on August 9, 2014, at the hands of Missouri police officer Darren Wilson, this "good boy" had been charged in 2013 with burglary first degree, armed criminal action, assault in 1st degree, causing serious physical injury, armed criminal action, etc.—just in a single year alone. Of course, the media remained silent about these realities while pushing the narrative of a White policeman killing an innocent Black boy for no reason.

In reality, Michael Brown robbed a store and proceeded to walk away down the middle of the street with his friend Dorian Johnson. Officer Wilson asked them to use the sidewalk. Instead of complying with the request, the two young men started to argue with the officer. During the exchange of words, Officer Wilson noticed a pack of cigarillos in Michael Brown's hand. Officer Wilson recalled that a radio dispatcher reported the theft of cigarillos from a nearby store. Officer Wilson confronted Michael Brown about the cigarillos. In response, Michael Brown reached into Officer Wilson's SUV, trying to seize his gun. A fight ensued. The gun went off.

Michael Brown started to run away, then he stopped, turned around, and started to run toward Officer Wilson. Michael Brown, a young man with a 6'4" stature and weighing 290 pounds, approached Officer Wilson in a threatening manner. Officer Wilson discharged his weapon several times. Regardless, Michael Brown kept running toward Officer Wilson. Officer Wilson's last shot to the head killed Michael Brown.

Following Dorian Johnson's false depiction of the incident, a thorough Justice Department investigation cleared Officer Wilson of any wrongdoing. However, Former President Obama's then Attorney General "Wingman" Eric Holder forced the Justice

Department to issue a report accusing the Ferguson police of "racial bias." No wonder Ferguson has become a false cause celebre for the radical extremist wing of the Democrat Party and its propaganda arm, the media.

The George Floyd case in Minneapolis is another proof of the destructive mindsets of Democrat politicians and the media, yet certain facts of his case are incontrovertible. On May 25, 2020, an employee of Cup Foods in Minneapolis called 911. He reported that a big Black man paid for cigarettes using a fake $20 bill. The employee said that the same person was sitting in his car and appeared "awfully drunk." Responding officers ordered George Floyd to exit his car. He physically resisted. The officers handcuffed him and simultaneously called for an ambulance because "he appeared to be suffering medical distress." Falsely claiming to be claustrophobic, George Floyd did not want to get into the back seat of the police car. Another struggle ensued. George Floyd was wrestled to the ground. Officer Chauvin tried to restrain the still struggling George Floyd by pressing his knee against his neck, and George Floyd died.

A heavyset man with a stature of 6'4" and weighing 223 pounds, George Floyd was a ruthless and violent criminal. As usual, the anti-Trump media and the leadership of the Democrat Party quickly seized the opportunity to accuse President Trump and the Republican Party of allegedly trying "to get away with murder." In this manner, a violent and hardened criminal suddenly metamorphosed into a martyr of "White racism."

In contrast, Officer Derek Chauvin has been hysterically described by Democrat politicians and Hollywood celebrities as subhuman, evil, and a White domestic terrorist, ripe to be publicly lynched, etc.

While the trial against the officers was still in progress, Maxine Waters travelled to Brooklyn Center, a Minneapolis suburb, and urged the already violent protesters to "stay on the street and get more active, more confrontational. We've got to make sure that they know that we mean business." As Jonathan Turley pointed out on Fox News, Maxine Waters charged that President Trump's January 6, 2021, call for his supporters to go to the Capitol to make their voices heard and "fight" for their votes was actual criminal incitement.

Alan Derschowitz, another eminent authority of criminal law likened Waters' attempt to influence the jury to the tactics of the Ku Klux Klan, "This was an attempt to intimidate the jury. It's borrowed precisely from the Ku Klux Klan of the 1930s and 1920s when the Klan would march outside courthouses and threaten all kinds of reprisals if the jury ever dared convict a white person or acquit a black person. And so, efforts to intimidate a jury should result in a mistrial with the judge, of course, wouldn't grant a mistrial because then he'd be responsible for the riots that would ensue, even though it was Waters who was responsible." As he predicted, Hennepin County Judge Peter Cahill rejected a motion for a mistrial from Chauvin's lawyer. However, the judge told the lawyer that he could submit articles about the remarks for an "appeal that may result in this whole trial being overturned."

Naturally, Speaker Pelosi disagreed. Rejecting calls to censure Maxine Waters, Pelosi opined that Waters' words were absolutely justified and appropriate. Another Democrat loud-mouth with no brains in the House of Representatives, New York Congresswoman Alexandria Ocasio-Cortez declared that the George Floyd murder trial was "not justice." As a former bartender and unquestionably highly qualified criminal law attorney without a law degree, she went on to pontificate about the trial thus, "That a family had to lose a son, brother, and father, that a teenage girl had to film and post a murder, that millions across the country had to organize and march just for George Floyd to be seen and valued is not justice. And this verdict is not a substitute for policy change."

Someone will have to tell this irredeemably incompetent and stupid member of the House of Representatives that George Floyd abandoned his family long before he died. Moreover, his family failed to teach him how to be a good and law-abiding member of an orderly society. Finally, a verdict in a criminal case is always about the guilt or innocence of a particular person or persons and should never be a political football.

While George Floyd was rapidly marching toward sainthood, Cecilia Regina, a Black woman, tweeted the following state-ment, "George Floyd was arrested and convicted of robbing and beating a PREGNANT BLACK WOMAN after breaking into her home. He wanted money and drugs, and when she didn't have either, he pointed a gun at her stomach." For evidence, she attached photos of the court record of his conviction as well as his criminal history that could have filled a small library. In conclusion, she pleaded with the protesters in Minneapolis, "STOP MARCHING FOR THIS MAN. STOP POSTING FOR HIM. HE WAS A MONSTER WHO TERRORIZED BW IN LIFE. DO NOT SUPPORT HIM WITH YOUR LABOR IN HIS DEATH. IF YOU DO, YOU ARE SUPPORTING A MAN WHO HATED AND HARMED BLACK WOMEN! YOU CANNOT HAVE IT BOTH WAYS THIS TIME. EITHER YOU ARE FOR THE SAFETY OF BLACK WOMEN OR YOU ARE SAYING THAT WE DON'T MATTER COMPARED TO BLACK MAN. SHARE, SHARE, SHARE."

Predictably, the square where he died was quickly named after George Floyd, the so-called "Saint" and "Martyr," at the intersection of E. 38 Street and Chicago Avenue in Minneapolis. A sign near the entrance of the square welcomes visitors to "A Sacred Space for Community, Public Griff, and Protest." The sign reminds everyone that this is the area where Floyd "took his last breath under the knee of" Mark Chauvin. The sign also urges visitors to "honor the space as a place to connect and grieve as caring humans." Moreover, it posts a special set of instructions for White people. Such visitors need to "decenter" and "come to listen, learn, mourn, and witness."

For good measure, the instructions continue thus, "Remember [Whites], you are here to support, not to be supported." White people are asked to "contribute to the energy of space rather than drain it." Any processing, whatever that means, must be brought to "other white folks" so that BIPOC (an acronym for Black and Indigenous People of Color) are not harmed. Finally, White people are encouraged to "engage rather than escalate, so that it can be a learning moment rather than a description." I think that such a confusing and fallacious message must rest by itself without any sane comment.

However, Cecilia Regina is an honest woman, and what she said is the real truth. Law-abiding Blacks have not been victimized by "White racism" or "systematic and institutionalized racism." Black criminals, however, victimize the entire nation because they sow fear in every state of the Union. In a democracy where the rule of law reigns, following the commands of members of law enforcement organizations is the most elementary responsibility of every person. Moreover, in a democracy, people have rights that come with responsibilities too. Finally, resistance to those commands is illegal and should be punished.

The fact that the trial of Derek Chauvin was a sham and a gross miscarriage of justice has also been proven by the public confession of one of the jurors, who was chosen despite wearing a Black Lives Matter shirt. Having vowed impartiality, Brandon Mitchell told syndicated radio host Erica Campbell that he wanted to serve on the Derek Chauvin jury to "see some things going differently." He added, "We gotta get out there and get into these avenues, get into these rooms to try to spark some change. Jury duty is one of those things—jury duty, voting. All of those things we gotta do." In closing, he also stated that the jurors were quickly ready to convict Derek Chauvin on all charges of second-degree murder, third-degree murder, and manslaughter.

As it turned out, Brandon Mitchell shamelessly lied to the judge. He also stated to Derek Chauvin's lawyer during questioning that he didn't know whether Derek Chauvin did anything wrong and that he believed the officer had no intention of harming anyone. However, a Facebook post in August 2020 by Travis Mitchell, Brandon Mitchell's uncle, shows the future juror sporting a Black Lives Matter hat and a T-shirt with the message "Get your knee off our necks." Even more importantly, *The Washington Times* reported in its May 5, 2021, issue that this monstrous liar wore the George Floyd-themed T-shirt not once, but at least twice in public.

Asked about his failing memory, juror 52, Travis Mitchell, defended himself thus, "I think they asked if I attended any protests for George Floyd or anything for police brutality. My answer was no because I hadn't." He later told WCCO-TV, "This particular march [where he wore the T-shirt in question] was more for voting, voter registration. Getting people out to get out and vote for the presidential election that was upcoming a couple of months afterward. [...] This was the only thing I attended." After his spurious defense, only one question remains. Is he really that stupid, or is he a shameful liar? Regardless, the utter illegality of the Derek Chauvin persecution has been in full display from the very beginning of the George Floyd affair. Either the United States of America is still a country governed by the rule of law, or justice is administered by a vengeful and dishonest mob. If the former is true, Derek Chauvin deserves a new and fair trial. In the case of the latter, it could be the beginning of the end for the United States of America as we know it.

Pointing out the numerous legal problems before and during the trial, Andrew C. MacCarthy opined on April 20, 2021, in the *National Review*, "The speedy nature of the decision [by the jury] could lead to problems for prosecutors in the appellate process." He also questioned the insufficient proof of intent in the two murder counts—felony murder and depraved-indifference homicide. He added, "I thought the evidence on the manslaughter count 'culpable negligence' for which it is unnecessary for prosecutors to prove criminal intent was daunting." In conclusion, Mr. MacCarthy expressed his doubt about whether Derek Chauvin got a fair trial.

In the case of the accidental shooting of Daunte Wright, the media and the same Democrat politicians again seized the opportunity to spread an outrageously false narrative. For starters, Daunte Wright was also a hardened criminal. Although only 20 years old, he was involved in two separate shooting incidents. In the first case, he and his friends were involved in a violent carjacking that left the owner of the car with a gunshot wound to his leg. In the second case, Wright shot Caleb Livingston in the head and left him permanently disabled outside a gas station in May 2019. When he was accidentally shot, the air freshener hanging on the frame of the interior mirror was not the cause of Daunte Wright's death as the media claimed.

As in the two previous cases, Daunte Wright killed himself. He was pulled over by the police because he had expired tags on his license plate. Following further checking, the police ascertained that he had an outstanding warrant for an assortment of misdemeanors and felonies. When the police tried to handcuff him, he resisted and pressed his body through the open door of his car. He wanted to escape. A 26-year veteran of the police force pulled her gun instead of her taser and shot him once in his upper body. While trying to then flee, he crashed his car. He died, and his girlfriend was injured. The sadness over his death is justified. The outrage of his parents and friends is understandable.

However, the repeat of the mayhem that gripped the nation several times before is misplaced. Daunte Wright was a problematic teenager. He dropped out of high school and fathered a child out of wedlock whom he could not support. A sadly familiar story with today's young Black males. His grieving father called him a "good boy." As many already noted, "good boys" do not commit multiple crimes. This so-called good boy was charged with aggravated burglary in December 2019 along with another man by the name Emajay Maurice. This good boy threatened a woman with a knife, choked her, and told her to give him her money or he would shoot her. His mother blamed everybody except her husband and herself. Instead of fervently looking for people to blame, they might want to look in the mirror and contemplate their own shortcomings as parents to a young man who thought he had only rights but no responsibilities.

The Black mayor of Brooklyn Center Mike Elliot reacted as expected. He immediately assured the mob that he is on their side and would comply with their demand to serve justice according to their desire. This, of course, means no due process and no impartial investigation. He already fired the city manager who criticized the mayor for rushing to judgment and also forced the police chief out of his job. It is worthwhile to note that these two summarily fired officials are Black. The mayor also prevailed upon the city council to pass a motion giving him command authority over the police department. Brooklyn Center is a small suburb just north of Minneapolis. In 2000, more than 70% of the city was White. Today, almost the same percentage are Black, Asian, and Latino.

After Daunte Wright's death, the usual script was followed by the usual mob—riots (mostly in Democrat controlled cities), mayhem, looting, police restraint, and media incitement. Needless to say, most Americans are sick and tired of this repeated rule of mob in their cities. Meanwhile, there is a burgeoning war on law enforcement. In 2020, 264 police personnel were killed— 96% more than 2019. Murder rates are skyrocketing in New York, Chicago, Atlanta, Portland, Los Angeles, San Francisco, and throughout Democrat-run cities across the United States of America.

Idiotically, Democrat politicians call for the abolition of the police and turning over their budgets to the homeless, unemployed, and other disadvantaged people. One of the idiots-in-chief, the self-described Palestinian Congresswoman Rashida Talib calls for "no more policing, incarceration, and militarization." To demonstrate why over 90% of Americans loathe Congress, Rashida Talib represents Detroit where the increase in the number of homicides went up 19% from 2019 to 2020. The number of non-fatal shootings increased by 53%. In her defense, the data in other big cities is even worse.

Clearly, the 240-year-old American civilization is in a crisis—a crisis artificially created by what I term as American idiots on the left fringes of society. These radical extremists enjoy not just a political cover by Democrat politicians but also their active support in acquiring absolute power over the large majority of American people. If for nothing else, this majority must finally rise and actively oppose those who are determined to destroy the country.

It appears that the list of false Black martyrs is endless. The most recent cause celebre of Black Lives Matter, Antifa, Maxine Waters, and her fellow idiots is a girl by the name of Ma'Khia Bryant from Columbus, Ohio. Proving that Democrat Senators are not smarter than their colleagues in the House of Representatives, Senator Sherrod Brown of Ohio mused, "While the verdict was being read in the Derek Chauvin trial, Columbus police shot and killed a sixteen-year-old girl. Her name was Ma'Khia Bryant. She should be alive right now." No word in Senator Brown's musing about why the police had to use deadly force and why her short life actually ended so tragically. Ayanna Pressley, another brain power of the so-called "Squad," also chimed in, "Black girls deserve girlhood uninterrupted. Black girls deserve to grow up and become women." Again, nothing about the actual context of the police shooting.

In reality, police officers were called to the scene one afternoon due to a report of someone attempting to stab others at home. That someone was Ma'Khia Bryant. As soon as the police arrived, they said Ma'Khia Bryant was observed tackling another female to the ground with what appeared to be a fairly big knife in her hand. In the video, the girl can be seen charging at another nearby female while raising the knife in her hand in the air. At which point, the officer fired multiple shots, fatally wounding Ma'Khia Bryant.

With the so-called Fourth Revolution on its way across the globe, Black Lives Matter is well into the process of digging an unbridgeable abyss between the majority of Americans, consisting not just of Whites but also a fairly small minority of Blacks. Glaringly, Black Lives Matter has been silent about the Black minority's own responsibilities to lift themselves out of their disadvantageous situation. Even more despicably, the organization has not spent the donations on improving the lot of the downtrodden people they allegedly represent. Reality is almost always unpleasant and even brutal, yet the leaders of Black Lives Matter do not want to deal with the daily struggles of many African Americans. What they really want is power and money for themselves. Everything else is immaterial for these unconscionable knights of "social justice" and "White racism".

Indeed, the case of Black Lives Matter co-founder Patrisse Cullors must stand out as incontrovertible evidence of and a serious warning about the base hypocrisy of these high priests of race hustlers. Having described herself repeatedly and proudly as a "trained Marxist," she bought a $1.4 million compound in the 88% White and 1.9% Black community of Topanga Canyon in Los Angeles County. Reporting about her "capitalist" habit in its February 11, 2021, issue, *The Washington Times* quotes comments from several individuals. Sports commentator Jason Whitlock sarcastically remarked, "She'll have her pick of white cops and white people to complain about. That's a choice, bro." The California Globe's Katy Grimes asked some fundamental questions too, "Was it ever really about improving black lives or just her own on the backs of BLM? And many are asking where the $1.4 came from?" More significantly, where did her reportedly $3.1 million real estate portfolio came from? Indeed, real Marxism at work in its totally sham ideological glory.

The ultimate insult against the intelligence of the American people that has been perpetrated by the Black Lives Matter organization has been the demand for reparations for slavery for all

Blacks. Based on the historical and ideological lies of the 1619 Project, the demand for ubiquitous reparations for Blacks extols ethnic pride mixed with radical hatred toward all other races. At its very root, the 1619 Project declares the collective guilt of Whites and the collective impunity of Blacks. This propaganda piece is full of disinformation and gives the lie to over 240 years of serious commemorations of the Black experience in the United States of America.

Almost exclusively sponsored and promoted by *The New York Times*, Chairman Arthur Sulzberger, Jr., opined that it is proper and timely to tell Black students about their perpetual victimhood in an incorrigibly racist country. What a positive and uplifting message for young African Americans! What a great motivation for these young people to study and strive for being excellent! What a wise exhortation for all of them to be good and productive citizens of the United States of America!

Yet according to the organization's leaders, reparations are not negotiable. However, what they really claim is eliminating any distinction between truth and lies. To illustrate the intellectual depravity of Black Lives Matter in this matter as well, the chancellor of the New York City school system, a Black woman by the name of Meisha Ross Porter, has reportedly attempted to force her staff to perform "Wakanda Forever" salutes to "Black Power." This salute was popularized by the movie *Black Panther* and involves crossing both arms across the chest with fists pointing upward. According to the movie, it's a symbol of

Black empowerment and a gesture of solidarity with the mythical African country Wakanda in which absolute political as well as social justice prevails in a utopian fashion.

Thus, the Declaration of Independence, the Constitution, and the almost two-and-a-half century of American history is nothing compared to a Hollywood movie full of imaginary nonsense and ideological garbage. These historical lies and many other similar misrepresentations have also been spread by notable public figures with golden tongues but little brain power, such as the Obamas, Al Sharpton, Jesse Jackson, Louis Farrakhan, and other ideologically and badly misguided false prophets of the "historical necessity" of "progress" of the Black race.

Not to be outdone, a so-called Critical Race Theory (CRT) movement has gained popularity among civil-rights lawyers and other assorted activists in academia. Officially established in 1989 at the first annual workshop on Critical Race Theory, CRT has become an integral part of neo-racist political organizations. Rooted in a superficial interpretation of Karl Marx's writing, who himself was an incorrigible racist and anti-Semite, CRT pretends to critically examine the law as it intersects with issues of race and simultaneously challenges existing mainstream approaches to racial justice.

In plain English, these so-called scholars claim that both the legal system as well as legal institutions are "inherently racist" and that race itself, instead of being biologically grounded and natural, is a socially constructed concept that is used by White people to further their economic and political interests at the expense of people of color. Having been born out of a primitive upsurge of extremely negative passions and biased cultic lies, Critical Race Theory at its core is nothing but a thoroughly false attempt at accommodating a tiny minority within a small minority to survive in a world in which they cannot compete.

Beyond its abuse of history, Critical Race Theory has been designed to replace the realities of the past, the present, as well as the future with a false religion-like reality with its pathologically infected sycophants existing under the authoritarian despotism of a few mentally unstable and even deranged leaders. For these intellectually misguided and ultimately betrayed people, realities are illusions and lies that they are fed incessantly to become normal political and social "realities." Tragically, history superabounds with examples of realities that have been challenged by "scientism" masquerading as science and with useful idiots that have been determined to alter the whole organization of societies.

What Critical Race Theory would mean in practice has been demonstrated by a pair of Ivy League medical professionals who called for giving medical preference to racial minorities. Bram Wispelwey and Michelle Morse are teachers at Harvard Medical School and practice at Brigham and Women's Hospital. They are well educated, well regarded in their profession, and hate-filled neo-racists. The two co-authored an article in the *Boston Review* in which they demanded their hospital provide "cash transfers and discounted or free care to black and latinx patients, and to prioritize these patients for cardiology admissions." For these two, the Hippocratic oath they swore to and the laws of the United States of America are obviously just words that carry no real-life meanings. Instead of delivering colorblind medical care, they state that "racist death panels are a good thing when we do it."

Proving these medical doctors should not practice medicine is a lecture by a certain Dr. Aruna Khilanani. A practicing New York City psychiatrist, she was invited to give a lecture by the Yale School of Medicine entitled "The Psychopathic Problem of the White Mind." To further promote her lecture, a flyer help-fully added that she would pontificate about how to "understand how white people are psychologically dependent on black rage." According to media reports, she did not disappoint her audi-ence. During the speech, she said she had fantasies of "unloading a revolver into the head of any White person" that got in her way. She also projected her blooming idiocy on the White race in general when she opined that "addressing racism assumes that White people can see and process what we are talking about, but they can't." Clearly, her lecture does not require any comments.

Just when unsuspecting sane people think Dr. Aruna Khilanani's professional idiocy cannot be trumped, out comes the most recent article of Dr. Donald Moss in *The Journal of the American Psychoanalytic Association*. Titled "On Having Whiteness," this monstrous idiot argues that White people possess an "entitled dominion" that enables the "hist" to wield power "without limit, force without restriction, violence without mercy," and increases one's desire to "terrorize." Furthermore, he states, "White people have a particular susceptibility" to the "parasitic" condition because "White pathology" renders its "hosts' appetites voracious, insatiable, and perverse." Finally, Dr. Moss, who serves on the faculties of both the New York Psychoanalytic Institute and the San Francisco Center for Psychoanalysis, offers an "effective" treatment that "consists of a combination of psychic and social-historical interventions. Such interventions can reasonably aim only to reshape Whiteness's infiltrated appetites—to reduce their intensity, redistribute their aims, and occasionally turn those aims toward the work of reparations." Again, no comment is necessary. However, the idiocy of pseudo-science, or no science at all, is clearly apparent.

The idiocy of Critical Race Theory with its "social justice," which in reality are serial anti-social injustices, lies in education. Audrey Conklin of Fox News reported on two Chicago-based professors gushing about teaching social justice as part of Critical Race Theory. Accordingly, Professor Gina Harris, who also serves on the Oak Park and River Forest High School school boards opined, "I mean, it's all social justice. All day, every day I get to talk about all the things I love." Her colleague with the same IQ, Professor Ralph Martire, chimed in, "The first three or four classes are devoted to philosophy of social justice and how to organize society. [...] We don't talk about one, you know, budgetary item. They're like, 'Oh, man. Professor Martire, this is a really weird way to teach a budget." The learned Professor

Martire's reply, "If you don't understand your values, you can't allocate resources among public priorities that are scarce, but all needed. Right?" A case when the students knew more than the teacher. Idiots are teaching sane people. Poor students! Poor parents! They are forced to pay through the nose for high tuition in order for their children to advance in the workplace!

All of this outrageous nonsense is justified by hapless Joe's executive orders about "advancing racial equity." This parsing of words tallies nicely with Marx's Class Struggle Theory that differentiates between "equality" for all and "equity"—the class-based and politically tainted preferential treatment for the ruling class. For these extreme neo-racist anarchists, even Martin Luther King's famous quote is just a piece of paper, "Not by the color of their skin but by the content of their character." Clearly, these two have no character and lack every human ability to work in their profession.

Thus, in the name of racial "equity" on his first day in office, the Doofus-in-Chief in the White House revoked President Trump's Executive Order No. 13950 for Combating Race and Sex Stereotyping of September 22, 2020, which stated the Critical Race Theory is rooted in the pernicious and false belief that America is an irredeemably racist and sexist country—that some people, simply on account of their race and sex, are oppressors and racial and sexual identities are more important than our common status as human beings and Americans. E.O. No. 13950 went on to quote from existing training materials being used by federal agencies in which the authors admonished "small group leaders to encourage employees to avoid narratives that Americans should be more color blind" or "let people's skills and personalities be what differentiates them."

This discombobulated thesis is also rooted in what the Communists in the Soviet Union and throughout Eastern Europe used to call "vulgar" Marxism, according to which ideologies are based on the ownership of the "means of production." Again, in plain English, capitalists create laws, social norms, and morality that suit their interests. Naturally, anyone who dares to disagree with this primitive interpretation of human history and the structure of societies is labeled a racist who supports "White privilege" and "systematic and institutionalized racism."

Clearly, CRT does not want a serious dialogue within the framework of a free and unprejudiced exchange of ideas. What they demand is confession of guilt by every non-Black individual and the uncritical acceptance of their politically, economically, and socially unworkable platform. As Allan Bloom so succinctly put it in his book *The Closing of the American Mind*, "Freedom of the mind requires not only, or not even specially, the absence of legal constraints, but the presence of alternative thoughts. The most successful tyranny is not the one that uses force to assure uniformity, but the one that removes the awareness of other possibilities."

It appears that no one has read the above-quoted passage from Allan Bloom's book at the American Bar Association. Under the title of "A Lesson on Critical Race Theory" and penned by Janel George on January 12, 2021, the author harks back to the 1960s to condemn racial oppression on the one hand and to justify CTR's despotic pseudo-ideology and authoritarian demands. The same untrue, uncompromising, and self-righteous mentality has also permeated the majority in the international community of like-minded European, Asian, African, and Australian intellectuals.

In this manner, instead of encouraging people of all ages to keep an open mind to their surroundings and the wider world, these neo-racist idiots attempt to force upon humanity indoctrination that contains nothing but complete and utter crap. Under the guise of fighting nonexistent "systematic and institutionalized racism," they strive with all their power to establish the neo-racist Communist dictatorship of a small and absolutely feckless minority. Harking back to the eight lost years of community organizer Barack Obama, they intone his neo-racist remarks, "The legacy of slavery, Jim Crow, discrimination in every institution of our lives—you know, that casts a long shadow, and that's still part of our DNA that's passed on. We're not cured of it. [...] Racism—we are not cured of it."

Barack, you are dead wrong! For starters, you received more White votes in 2008 than Democrat candidate John Kerry did in 2004. Then in 2012, in spite of your utter incompetence, the majority of the American people, most significantly Whites, re-elected you for another four-year term. Moreover, you and your family have become very rich on you and Michelle milking your past presidency to the maximum. Finally, you, Barack, missed many opportunities to prove that "systematic and institutionalized racism" is nothing but the Big Lie of your party.

For the purposes of this book, it is sufficient to remind the readers of the infamous case of Professor Henry Louis Gates. Without even rudimentarily being familiar with the events surrounding this case, Barack, as a lawyer, opined thus, "The Cambridge police acted stupidly." Translation, "Cops systematically engage in unlawful anti-Black racial profiling." Although Barack Obama is not the smartest man that ever inhabited this earth, he should have known that there is no evidence of anti-Black "systematic and institutionalized racism." However, he declared a lie to be the truth because Black outrage means Black votes for the Democrats.

Barack Obama's then Vice President and the current President, Joe Biden, who was elected on his self-declared "moderation" and his promise that "my whole soul is in this: Bringing America together, uniting our people, and uniting our nation." In reality, on his first day in office, he turned against everything he solemnly promised during his campaign to the people. From day one, he and his administration have mischaracterized and outright lied about his predecessor's policies between 2017 and 2021.

Clearly, he has betrayed his high-minded aspirations. In an opinion piece published by Tribune Media Services, Victor Davis Hanson wrote that Biden leads the most radical left-wing movement in U.S. history. Intimating that Biden will "accelerate the current hard-left trajectory" with his open borders, blanket amnesties, cancelation of the Keystone XL pipeline, promotion of the Green New Deal, hard-left appointments, etc., he predicts that Biden will most likely fail.

Going beyond Victor Davis Hanson's apt criticism, the Biden administration is hell-bent to repeat Barack Obama's many mistakes, especially in foreign policy. The hysterical fury over the assassinations of Qasem Soleimani and Mohsen Fahrizadeh by the hopelessly pro-Muslim and anti-Israel John Brennan, Obama's counterterrorism "Tsar" and CIA Director, has been echoed by Secretary of State Antony Blinken who emphasized the universality of human rights thus, "All people are entitled to these rights, no matter where they're born, what they believe, whom they love, or any other characteristic." The enemies of the United States of America, including lethal terrorists too? Hence, the return at all cost to the Iran deal and the "cancelling" of President Trump's historical achievements in the greater Middle East. Against all the facts, Iran-appeasers and bash-Israel-firsters have gained the upper hand in Biden's pseudo-reality world.

Then there is the Afghanistan fiasco showcasing the idiocy of demented Joe Biden and the incompetence of his minions, including the current military leadership as well as the intelligence agencies. While the orderly withdrawal of the remaining American military has been royally botched, demented Joe enjoyed his not-so-well-deserved vacation, and his irredeemably incompetent deputy was hysterically laughing in Singapore when asked about Afghanistan. To make matters even worse, his Secretary of Defense and the Chairman of the Joint Chiefs of Staff have been busy re-educating the entire American military by ordering a ubiquitous "stand down" to address the "challenge of extremism in the ranks."

To demonstrate the joint idiocy of Lloyd Austin and Mark Milley, DoD's spokesman John Kirby attempted to mitigate the damage by saying, "The vast majority of men and women who serve in uniform and the military are doing so with honor, integrity, and character and do not espouse the sort of beliefs that lead to the kind of conduct that can be so detrimental to good order and discipline and in fact is criminal." Proving that his stupidity knows no limits, the Secretary of Defense decided to challenge his spokesman's words by stating, "No matter what it is, it is. [...] not an insignificant problem and has to be addressed." Thus, political correctness is more important than the overall situation in Afghanistan on the eve of the American military's departure and the consequences of the Taliban's Blitzkrieg for the United States of America and the rest of the world.

Tragically, this eternal struggle between Truth and Lies has not been limited to the Black minority. Under the slogans of "no more genocide" and "all colonizers are bastards," the so-called Pan-Indigenous People's Liberation (PIPL) network with the active assistance of the American Indian Movement, which has called for a "national decolonial day of action," pulled down a statue of Christopher Columbus outside of Pittsburgh. Not to be outdone, a mob in Portland, Oregon, tagged local markets and a monument dedicated to the veterans of the Civil War, as well as the Mexican, Spanish and Indian Wars with anti-colonial rhetoric. The West Coast states of Washington, Oregon, and California witnessed similar efforts in the thousands.

Chicago, the largest city in the midwestern region, saw an attempt to remove the statue of President William McKinley. Another phantom organization that calls itself LANDBACK states, "Through the revitalization of our Indigenous ceremonies, culture, languages, and life ways, we will continue to strengthen our identity and break free from the oppressive systems that disconnect us from achieving the healing growth and connection to spirit that is integral for us as Indigenous people." What a fabulous political strategy! What a well-thought out and defined set of policies toward political and economic freedom and existential security! Finally, what a practical guide toward national prosperity!

Not to be outdone, the Mayor of Washington, D.C., Muriel Bowser, has also joined the party of this idiocy. In 2020, she established a commission with the goal of studying whether to "remove, relocate, or contextualize" various monuments, schools, and other infrastructure in pursuit of her stated objective to align D.C. with "D.C. Values." Besides the fact that the word contextualize is totally inappropriate for the commission's mission and not clarifying what she means by "D.C. Values," the Mayor's incompetent tinkering with history surely would not significantly improve the standard of living for the inhabitants of the federal capital city. Clearly, by such and similar token actions, she hopes to hide her overall incompetence and her utter cluelessness regarding policies to improve the lot of the majority of Blacks across the city.

Most recently, Chicago Mayor Lori Lightfoot, otherwise an absolutely incompetent public servant and a raging racist, stated that on her two-year anniversary in office, she would grant one-on-one interviews to non-Whites only. Proving that she is a true follower of Adolf Hitler, she declared, "[I am indeed] exclusively providing one-on-one interviews with journalists of color." Claiming huge pressure from "Black and Brown community leaders" that media coverage was biased, she went on to state, "So, here I am, like so many other Black women before me, having to call your attention to this problem."

To elevate her racist hypocrisy to new heights, she justified her order to the Chicago Police Department to prohibit people from protesting on the block where she lives saying, "I think that residents of this city, understanding the nature of the threats that we are receiving on a daily basis, on a daily basis, understand I have a right to make sure that my home is secure." In light of the violence that has held the rest of the inhabitants of the city hostage to mostly Black criminals, no commenting on her professed victimhood status is needed. Perhaps, she should be reminded that the right to safety is universal. Everyone deserves safety, especially in his or her home. Not surprisingly, Chicago's

Fraternal Order of Police issued a vote of no confidence in Mayor Lori Lightfoot, citing poor work conditions and the cancellation of a march for fallen officers due to the coronavirus pandemic.

Regrettably, such and similar examples abound across the United States of America. The mayors of New York City, Boston, Atlanta, Chicago, Seattle, Portland, San Francisco, Denver, and Los Angeles have proven again and again that their ingrained ideological idiocies always top sanity in their decision making. Among them, the most outlandish have been the gutting of the police budgets in their respective domains and the curtailing of the rights of all uniformed personnel. In this alternative world, social identity defines political identity. Clearly, this is an unfailing recipe for dividing a person from another person and fragmenting entire societies until they are totally destroyed. These cult-like miniscule collections of people are also imbued with deep-seated and irrational hatred. Moreover, they are suffering pathological limitations on their intellectual faculties to come to grips with reality. Thus, they are always bound to replace reality with their fabrications, inventions, lies, and concoctions.

To top this avalanche of idiotic statements, one should wonder whether Dr. Rochelle Walenski, Director of the Center for Disease Control (CDC) is fit to be roaming the corridors of the federal bureaucracy freely instead of being confined to a closed mental hospital. In her deranged state of mind, Ms. Walenski stated that over the past year, the COVID-19 epidemic has "illuminated iniquities [...] and revealed for all of America a known, but often unaddressed, epidemic impacting public health: racism." Her justification is even more idiotic, "What we know is this: racism is a serious public health threat that directly affects the well-being of millions of Americans […][and] as the nation's leading public health agency, CDC has a critical role to play to address the impact of racism on public health."

Ms. Walenski is a political hack and not a serious professional. Has she and her organization conducted thorough research on the impact of so-called racism on public health, or has she only rushed to satisfy the political fashion of the day? Did she really mean that the racist Chinese dictatorship mostly targeted and sickened minorities, especially Blacks? Of course, her solutions are pouring more and more money at the so-called "problems" intended to "serve as a catalyst for public and scientific discourse around racism and health." No further comments are needed to prove that Ms. Walenski has lost her mind, provided that she had any at all.

And then there is Biden's newest "epidemic" called gun violence. His April 7, 2021, press conference, in which he again showed worrisome signs of advanced dementia, was full of blatant factual errors and outrageous lies. The most glaring of those was his contention that there is a "gun show loophole" in the laws that his executive order will close. Again, the utter lie of his statement was thoroughly rebuffed by David Lutz in his insightful article where he stated, "Biden's false remarks on gun show background checks gets a pass from some fact-checkers."

Biden's hypocrisy is even more stunning by nominating Kristen Clarck to head the Department of Justice's (DOJ) Civil Rights Division. At a conference she organized in April 1999, she and all the speakers defined cop-killers and violent criminals as "political prisoners" or "POWs," provided they were Black. Understandably, these "political prisoners" do not deserve the death penalty at all, such as Mumia Abu-Jamal, Mutulu Shakur, Sundiata Acoli and Tom Manning, in addition to other radical extremist criminals. Of course, Assata Shakur, who was convicted of murdering a New Jersey state trooper and hiding in one of Obama's and Biden's favorite dictatorships in Cuba, was hailed as a saint of Black liberation. Clearly, the hypocrisy is mind numbing. Unconditional respect for Black and Hispanic hardened criminals is expected while extreme loathing for normal, law-abiding people is deemed appropriate.

For these antisocial psychopaths, all normal people are enemies because their thinking is ultimately based on their closed-minded racist mentality. Finally, this kind of racist identity politics forces Whites, Blacks, Hispanics, Asians, and others into a hostage situation in which movements, interactions, and communications are strictly forbidden among them. Those who violate this racially induced political and spiritual terrorism are called traitors or even worse by the racially pure praetorian guard of identity politics.

Indeed, no dialogue, compromise, or understanding could be had with these persons hopelessly blinded by their irrational hatred. For them, their alternative universe means power. Absolute power is the real reason they develop two sets of rules—one for themselves and another for the rest of the people. For them, it is self-evident that they are innocent, and those who do not identify with their Kafkaesque/Orwellian worldview are guilty.

Sadly, this is the illusory framework for the sick world of these mentally ill individuals. Their unreal world is supported by their self-created theology of identity politics which is the new racism of the 21st century. In the same spirit, the main religious precept of this theology is the so-called "Cancel Culture." The identity politics and Cancel Culture that jointly comprise the terror of "WOKEISM" are about the total destruction of the historical roots of a community, an entire nation, and the whole of humanity. The Wokeists' extreme ideological persecution of the overwhelming majority of Americans with the guilty collaboration of the media and academia is a disgraceful failure of the United States of America as a country as well as its three branches of government.

Apparently, they individually as well as collectively have not read the late Pastor Martin Niemoller's famous poem about the individual's responsibility to oppose Hitler's genocidal authoritarianism, "First, they came for the Communists, and I did not speak out because I was not a Communist. Then they came for the Socialists, and I did not speak out because I was not a Socialist. Then they came for the trade unionists, and I did not speak out because I was not a trade unionist. Then they came for the Jews, and I did not speak out because I was not a Jew. Then they came for me, and there was no one left to speak out for me."

Fast forward to 2021. Wokeism is obsessed with race, racial identity, and sexual aberrations. In this broader sense, Wokeism is the new National Socialism of Adolf Hitler and his greater Germany between 1933 and 1945 and Stalin's cruel Communism between 1924 and 1953. The symbolic and real book-burning campaigns, indiscriminate toppling of statues, condemnation of the classics, designation of sciences as the proofs of "White supremacy", rejection of theatrical and musical classics as "White oppression", and the criticism of the Bible as the source of all evils, including slavery, discrimination against women, and base racism, all are reminders of the National Socialists and the Communist thugs and their ruthless acts against humanity.

Weaponizing skin color and racial identity as identifying attributes of one's DNA are the real political and social plagues of today's world. Clearly, what Wokeism generates is ubiquitous fear that turns every human community into a spiritual and physical graveyard. This dire picture of the present and the future is compounded by the fact that this catastrophe has been brought upon mankind by fanatic idiots with either no education at all or with superficial understanding of the world and the biased members of the media who are bullying people into silence or into political correctness day in and day out.

In this manner, the floodgate of idiocy has been forced wide open by these fanatics of the new racism. Paraphrasing Pastor Niemoller, these American idiots first came for Republican presidents' nominees for the Supreme Court in the late 1980s. Then, they came for the classic children's books, such as *Babar the Elephant*, H.A. Rey's *Curious George* books, Disney's *Peter Pan, Dumbo, Aristocats, Lady and the Tramp*, and *The Jungle Book*, Dr. Seuss' Geisel literary masterpieces, and *Swiss Family Robinson*.

The first book was criticized for its alleged "celebration of colonialism" because the elephant in the book returns from his journey outside Africa to "civilize" his fellow animals. In the case of the second book, a White man takes a monkey home with the intention to "demean Africans and especially African Americans." In *Dumbo*, the crows "pay homage to racist minstrel shows." *Peter Pan* "portrays native people in a stereotypical manner that reflects neither the diversity of native peoples nor their authentic cultural traditions. Peter and the Lost Boys engage in dancing, wearing headdresses, and other exaggerated tropes.

In *Swiss Family Robinson*, the pirates "appear in yellow face and are dressed in an exaggerated and inaccurate manner with top knot hairstyles, queues, robes and overdone facial make-up and jewelry, reinforcing their barbarism and otherness." Dr. Seuss was accused of "racist and insensitive imagery." To up the ante of irredeemable idiocy, Dr. Seuss was also condemned for his "racial transgressions across his entire publishing career." To pay homage to the anti-gender stereotyping fellow travelers, Stan and Jan Berenstain were also ridiculed for their claim that "I'm a father. I'm a he. A father's something you could be. I'm a mother. I'm a she. A mother's something you could be."

Never mind that of all these warriors of the Nazis' "entartete Kunst" (degenerate art) were, until most recently, contradicted by such luminaries of the "fundamental transformation" of the United States of America as Barack and Michelle Obama, Nancy Pelosi, Chuck Schumer, and their lunatic comrades. Prior to having seen the light of Wokeism at the end of their tunnel vision, they have praised all of the above-mentioned authors as wholesome for children as well as humanity.

Then they came for the sciences. Indeed, Black high school teachers as well as their colleagues at colleges and graduate schools declared mathematics, physics, chemistry, etc., the products of evil "White supremacy" that must be canceled too. Philosophy, history, arts, literature, etc., are equally evil and must be eliminated from the curriculum. Their collective guilt is that the brains behind all of those achievements were housed overwhelmingly inside White and not Black bodies.

Then they came for universal history too. Obviously, all conquerors, starting with the Egyptian Pharaohs, the Persian Kings, the Roman Emperors, and their successors, were colonizers. Discoverers, such as Cristopher Columbus and his colleagues, were racist demons who brought the inferior culture of the White man to the highly developed civilizations of the African tribes and the land of Native Indians in the entire

American continent. American presidents, starting with George Washington and temporarily ending with Donald Trump, naturally promoted shameless White racism to the detriment of the Black minority. On the other side of the Atlantic, Winston Churchill was declared the epitome of a racist politician.

Then they came for religion too. Since there is slavery in the Bible and discrimination against women and non-Jews, the Old Testament, called the TANACH by the Jewish people, must be destroyed forever. The New Testament is also a product of "White supremacy." Depicting Jesus as White when he was Black in actuality is a sin that cannot be tolerated. Hence, out with the "White supremacist" New Testament too. Question: What about the Quran? What about the spiritual books and utterances of Buddhism, Hinduism, Shintoism, etc.?

Then they came for the United States of America in its entirety. The Declaration of Independence, the Constitution, the flag, the national anthem, any symbol of the Confederacy, and everything else that defines the country were declared relics of "White supremacy" and "systematic and institutionalized racism" by these extremist and destructive minorities.

Antifa, Black Lives Matter, and other like-minded Fascist/ National Socialist/ Marxist/Stalinist anarchist organizations have occupied entire city blocks across the Pacific and Atlantic coastlines by establishing so-called "autonomous zones." Signs declaring that "You are leaving the United States" have been erected with the tacit approval of mayors and city councils. The equally irresponsible media with their idiotic staff have celebrated those nonsensical and lawless acts by calling them peaceful festivals and harmless expressions of dissent. All of these organizations and people have been masquerading as Democrats led by none other than President Biden. Pushing through an avalanche of executive orders in record time, his reversals of his predecessor's immigration and environmental policies and his politicized redistribution of wealth among blue and red states as well as among the different stratas of the population are founded on the unadulterated teachings of failed Marxism.

Clearly, the Democrat Party has totally submitted to the Fascist, National Socialist, and radical Marxist demands of these dangerous lunatics. Even the military and the federal and state law enforcement agencies have been forced to bow to the false and distorted interpretation of history by a minority who strives to ban all history and culture of which they disapprove.

Looking for new recruits, the CIA has created a slew of recruitment videos. One of those videos characterized by the CIA itself as "Humans of CIA" features a so-called "Latina" officer who identifies as a "cisgender millennial." Since the video is designed to attract a more diverse pool of candidates," she says with genuine enthusiasm in her voice, "I am a woman of color. I am a mom. I am a cisgender millennial who has been diagnosed with generalized anxiety disorder. I am intersectional, but my existence is not a box-checking exercise."

Having watched the full video that is rich with this and other diversity nonsense, I am reminded of a joke in Hungary about the CIA and the Soviet Union from the early 1970s. The joke goes like this: the CIA prepares an agent for years to be employed as a spy in the Soviet Union. After learning about history, culture, customs, etc., the prospective agent is sent to a Russian language school. He graduated with flying colors. The day comes when he is declared fit to start his job. In Moscow, he goes to a restaurant and orders lunch in flawless Russian. When the waitress brings the main course, he thanks her profusely. The waitress looks at him and says, "You are not Russian." The agent goes to Leningrad (renamed St. Petersburg after 1990) and repeats his Moscow routine. The waitress again asks him about the country he came from. It goes this way for a while. Finally, the agent asks a Russian, "Why do you say that I am not Russian?" His answer, "Because your skin color is black."

The moral of this joke is unequivocal. History is based on facts that cannot be changed according to the ideological desires of tiny minorities. One can dislike history, but one is not entitled to deny the existence of the past. As George Santayana so aptly remarked, "Those who cannot remember the past are condemned to repeat it." Paraphrasing the Spanish philosopher, Churchill echoed the same wisdom in the House of Commons in a 1948 speech, "Those who fail to learn from history are condemned to repeat it."

Meanwhile, the rest of the world is watching—the Free World with genuine concern and the multitude of undemocratic/illiberal regimes with unrestrained glee, universally known by the German word of Schadenfreude. According to at least half of the American people, Joseph R. Biden won the presidential election under extremely suspicious circumstances. Starting with the illegal modifications of election laws in key battleground states by executive orders controlled by the Democrats and continuing with suspending counting in regions where the sitting president was ahead until new ballots were repeatedly discovered in miraculous and mysterious ways during the next several days and even weeks. Indeed, for the unbiased observers the many frauds perpetrated by the Biden campaign were self-evident.

For those versed in the Constitution, the breach of Article 2, Section 1 provision that electoral laws can be made only by state legislatures is clear. Governors, state courts, etc., shall not have a role in changing those laws. Moreover, the Fourteenth Amendment and its Equal Protection Clause was also repeatedly violated. Although the state and federal courts, including the Supreme Court, jointly decided to stay out of the dirty politicization of the election process, the final tallies of all the votes cast raise a huge red flag concerning the veracity of the results. To start with, almost all of the numbers are a first in U.S.A. history. The 159,633,396 total votes is the largest turnout in American history. The second largest number was around 140 million. Biden won by 81,283,098 votes, again, a first in American history.

And so on and so forth. What is clear from these numbers is that the 2020 presidential election was also the most corrupt in American history.

For these reasons, it is no wonder that pollster Scott Rasmussen penned a column in which he quoted Joseph Stalin, "Those who cast the votes decide nothing. Those who count the votes decide everything." In this column, Rasmussen urged then Vice President Pence to exclude the results from every battleground state where the 2020 election results were contested when he appeared before Congress. In conclusion, he stated, "The President's [Donald Trump's] position going into January 2021 is thus considerably stronger than the mainstream media would like to admit." Continuing his argument, Rasmussen said, "There is constitutional language and historical precedent that gives his Vice President the unilateral power to decide the outcome of our contested election." Indeed, almost all Republicans and a sizable number of independents believe the elections were stolen and therefore Joe Biden is an illegitimate president.

Regardless whether the elections were stolen or not by the Democrats, Joe Biden and his administration will fail. His first 10 months have created nothing but ubiquitous chaos and violence. Voters' remorse has already begun to set in. The fact that the Democrat Party, the media, and Big Tech screwed them up becomes clearer by the day. The result will hopefully be that the American voters will return to the country's founding principles of small government, individual liberties, and democracy as its core identity. Only such a return to the Constitution will lead to achieving national unity of purpose and internal peace within the Republic.

For this to happen, there is an urgent case to be made for nationwide voting reform. The first steps have already been made in the state of Georgia with the signing of SB 202 into law on March 25, 2021. The expected disinformation campaign spearheaded by the White House itself is convincing proof that Democrats are not interested in a fair and workable voting system. Beginning with the childish claim that Georgia's voting law would block voters from accepting food and water while they are waiting in line at polling stations to the usual racist charges of "Jim Crowism" of disenfranchising minorities, the laundry list of Democrat lies is endless.

In reality, according to *The Dispatch*, an anti-Trump online outlet, "Attempts by prominent Democrats—including the president—to tie SB 202 to the Jim Crow era are incredibly disingenuous. For starters, the bill actually expands voting access for most Georgians, mandating precincts hold at least 17 days of early voting—including two Saturdays with Sundays optional—leading up to the election." Moreover, "Voting locations during this period must be open for at least eight hours and can operate between 7:00 a.m. and 7:00 p.m." And for good measure, the comparison, "Several states [including Biden's home state of Delaware which will not implement it until 2022] do not currently allow any in-person early voting, and plenty, like New Jersey, offer far fewer than 17 days." However, what SB 202 is trying to prevent is the recurrence of widespread cheating and other blatant shenanigans committed by the Democrats in November 2020 to steal the election.

The state of Florida will be next to enhance election integrity. On April 28, 2021, the House of Representatives voted 77-40 for a bill that will require signature verification for voters, provided by a "wet signature" physically signed on paper kept on file. It also revises distance limits for people at polling places or early voting sites and related sites, monitors ballot drop boxes by election workers, and introduces ID requirements for dropping of ballots. The bill also includes limitations on who can return a finished mail-in ballot, prevents election officials from entering consent agreements, and requires voters to submit yearly requests for mail-in ballots. No doubt this House version will be approved by the state Senate.

In Texas, the election-reform bill has initially been obstructed by the Democrat members in the House of Representatives. Childishly fleeing the state, they wanted to make a dramatic stand against the bill. However, what started as drama ended as a joke. They returned, and a bill was passed as intended.

To prove idiotic perseverance against all odds has become a permanent Democrat virtue, the House Democrats, passed a voting rights act on August 24, 2021, strictly along party lines (219-212) and named after the late Representative John Lewis. H.R. 4, the John Lewis Voting Rights Act, empowers the Department of Justice to judge whether a state voting bill is discriminatory or not. If the DoJ believes, even arbitrarily, that it does, the states need to get the DoJ's approval before making any changes to elections. However, the House version goes even further. Designed to counter the Supreme Court ruling that made it harder to challenge voting changes, it authorizes the DoJ to potentially overrule the Supreme Court.

The best solution to stem the tide of lawless manipulations and electoral fraud of the elections is to introduce the nationwide mandatory requirement of voter ID. Georgia's SB 202 requirements are contained in Section 21-2-417 of state law. It does require voters to present photo identification while voting. Accepted forms of ID include Georgia driver's licenses or ID cards, U.S. passports, and U.S. military ID. Voters can obtain a free voter ID card from any county registrar's office or Department of Driver Services Office. However, voters who do not have photo ID while voting may cast provisional ballots. Clearly, the artificial and politically motivated outrage over SB 202 is totally unjustified. Charges of voter suppression, White manipulation, and racism are absolutely bogus.

As of December 2020, 35 states enforced or were scheduled to begin enforcing voter identification requirements. On the other side of the ledger is California, that according to the Office of the California Secretary of State, "in most cases, California voters are not required to show identification at their polling place." Washington, D.C., is even more permissive. The capital city does not require identification from most voters. In the same vein, Illinois does not require voters to present identification while voting. Voters in Maine do not have to present identification at the polls. Democrat-controlled Maryland belongs to the same permissive group of states. Obviously, Massachusetts cannot stay behind the above-listed states. Minnesota, being a Democrat-controlled state, does not require photo identification either, and Nevada also belongs in the same category. New York does not require voters to present identification at the polls. Oregon is a vote-by-mail state. Pennsylvania has also dispensed with voter ID while voting. In Washington state, voters cast their ballots overwhelmingly by mail as well without the requirement to present an ID.

The joke that politicians want to be buried in Chicago so they can remain active in politics after they die regrettably still has merit in America. From the "voting dead" to other forms of voter fraud and voter intimidation, elections in the United States of America have been tainted with recurring suspicions of massive lawlessness on an industrial scale. The criminal manipulations and the politically motivated falsification of electoral rolls have always provided ample opportunities for voter fraud. This enduring problem should be of the highest concern for Congress, the Executive Branch, and the Judiciary. For these three branches of government, free and fair elections should be their top priority.

Coupled with the new Wokeism, the American people must also be interested in preventing democratic backsliding into a corrupt election process with fraudulent results. Therefore, reducing voter fraud is absolutely necessary to re-establish trust in American democracy. The problems of fictional voters and vote manipulation will only be solved by cleaning up local electoral rolls, creating a central registry, and improving electronic solutions for registration and voting. Since the Judiciary, including the Supreme Court, has repeatedly proven they are reluctant to dirty their hands with messy politics, the focus must be on prevention rather than litigation. Finally, bipartisan or even independent monitoring of the transportation of ballots must be ensured as well. Without the implementation of such additional measures, the danger of fictional ballots defeating real ones will shift even further toward unrealistic election results.

Conversely, the House of Representatives previously passed a companion bill to H.R.4, H.R. 1, named the For People Act, which has advanced to the Senate. Calling H.R. 1 the "universal fraud act," Senator Ted Cruz compared the law to the Democrats' numerous attempts to suppress the Civil Rights Movement of the 1950s. The donor disclosure provision of H.R. 1 is exactly the same as the abuse of the similar provision pushed aggressively in the 1950s in which Democrat governors and state attorneys general demanded that the National Association of Colored People (NAACP) divulge its supporters' names as a condition for operating within their states. Thus, H.R. 1—on a party line vote—made donor disclosure a national requirement under federal law. In sum, H.R. 1 is fundamentally rewriting the rules of American politics and campaign finance laws to guarantee Democrat control and the White House beyond 2022.

In order to accomplish these objectives, H.R. 1 puts Washington, D.C., in charge of running elections. Moreover, H.R. 1 mandates the financing of political campaigns with taxpayer dollars. Finally, H.R. 1 weaponizes federal agencies to target and silence Republicans and other conservative organizations as well as their donors. Yet, H.R. 1 goes even further as States will be required to automatically register any eligible voter based on inaccurate, duplicative federal databases, institute Election Day and online voter registration, and provide "no fault" absentee ballots, meaning voters could cast an absentee ballot for basically any reason they choose. To add insult to injury, H.R. 1 also changes the Federal Election Commission (FEC) from a panel of six to five members, ensuring that one political party controls the enforcement of the "For the People Act." Even more outrageously, H.R. 1 eliminates voter ID laws across the nation.

On the Senate side, the majority leader could not be charged for sitting idly on his laurels. As its House version, SR-1 promotes election fraud, gross government interference, and legalized corruption by elected politicians. Otherwise, SR-1 is the mirror image of H.R.-1 and 4, its bastard kins in the House of Representatives.

Encouragingly, the majority of Americans are beginning to realize the sweeping changes H.R. 1 has introduced include "confusion, chaos, fraud, and litigation." As Ronn Blitzer reported on Fox News, a new report examines "potentially severe consequences that House Democrats' voting reform bill H.R. 1 could have on states across the country, including ones that already have progressive laws on the books." The Honest Elections Project also notes that "14 states would have to institute no-excuse absentee voting" and be forced to "develop a system that would automatically place voters on an absentee list." The same report also criticizes the requirement of same-day voter registration. In conclusion, the report states, "If H.R. 1 is adopted, voters across the nation and in states across the political spectrum would see their election system upended. In their place would come strict mandates from Washington, novel voting systems, impossible deadlines, and the threat of costly lawsuits, if and when states fail to implement them."

The cumulative effect of this dire situation domestically is the erosion of trust in democracy, while internationally, the effect is the precipitous decline of the image of the United States of America as the leader of the Free World, especially the leaders of the People's Republic of China and the Russian Republic. Xi Jinping and Vladimir Putin are seasoned politicians. They are certainly not fooled by the extremely biased American and foreign media gushing over Joe Biden as a strong visionary leader. They rather believe their eyes, ears, and the reports of their intelligence services. Consequently, all of their information can only lead to a single conclusion—Joe Biden is not in charge and is suffering from an advanced case of dementia.

Their verdicts of Biden's Vice-President are even more disrespectful. They know that Kamala Harris was not selected because of her outstanding intellect but on her sex and the color of her skin. In fact, neither hapless Joe nor incompetent Kamala have ever had an original idea of their own. Throughout their less than mediocre careers, they both have been shameless plagiarists who stole entire speeches and passages of works from others as their own without any moral qualms. Therefore, they also understand that he and she are not and will never become competent leaders of the United States of America.

Moreover, they know the United States of America is deeply divided and its government is rudderless and perhaps fatally adrift. After calling Putin a "killer," the Russian President challenged hapless Joe to a debate about U.S. history. President Xi Jinping's foreign minister and his staff had a field day in Alaska by berating the woefully inexperienced Anthony Blinken and his companions about how corrupt, racist, evil, and irredeemably sinister the United States of America is. For the record, those were the exact adjectives that hapless Joe, his party, and his campaign cohorts used to describe the present state of American society.

Proving that WOKEISM for the Democrats is a zero-sum political game, the best illustration is their inhuman, immoral, and lawless campaign surrounding illegal immigration. Stripped of bogus political, economic, legal, and cultural narratives along with selective outrage, pseudo-realities, and linguistic falsehoods, the liberal progressives claim that illegal immigration, which they euphemistically call "migration," is also the product of White people's oppression of Central and South America is blatantly false. In reality, the ones who actually oppressed the people of the southern part of the American continent for centuries are the indigenous culture of "Caudillismo," the feudalistic mentality of authoritarian exercise of unbridled political power. From the successive rule of military juntas to the self-serving Communism of Juan Peron, the misery of the Latin American people has been of their own making. Yes, they are victims. However, they are not the victims of "Yankee" exploitation, but instead, they are the victims of their authoritarian and corrupt leaders as well as their own slavish mentality.

Moreover, the eternal backwardness of the southern hemisphere gives lie to the liberal/progressives' other fallacy which is "multiculturalism." In reality, cultures are different, and they are definitely not equal. There are and always have been superior and inferior cultures throughout history. Superior cultures have thrived, while inferior cultures have stagnated and died. The unvarnished truth is that the abiding majority of states in the world are in deep crises. Yet, the states of the southern hemisphere are in a multitude of hopeless domestic and international crises. No amount of money and no allotment of "American" values can turn the gloom of the western hemisphere around within a reasonable timeframe.

The liberal progressives have argued incessantly that open borders and unregulated migration is the only way to reduce world poverty. Of course, this argument is missing the problem again by thousands of miles. Allowing people of all nations to move freely will only create universal chaos. It certainly will not solve the problems of the most badly functioning states. It will only perpetuate uncertainty, insecurity, and ubiquitous misery. To wit, putting the so-called "White oppressors" in charge of solving the problems created by others is also the ultimate irony of the beliefs of the open border advocates.

President Biden, who has never had an original and realistic idea of his own, multiplied his administration's numerous problems by bowing to the extremist wing of the Democrat Party concerning illegal immigration. Having cancelled President Trump's policies on illegal immigration, including the unlawful stop of the border wall construction as being un-American and inhuman, with an avalanche of rushed and typically mindless executive orders, hapless Joe and his incompetent Secretary of Homeland Security have had to eat crow and restore most of the policies that his predecessor put in place. From criminal organizations' fabulous enrichment to the material and sexual exploitation of the mostly dirt-poor and uneducated illegal immigrants, the short-lived glorious apex of the Biden administration's

"American" and "humanitarian" open border policies are already in spectacular shambles.

Wokeism is a pseudo-religion invented by a bunch of anti-social psychopaths, such as the neo-racist Black Lives Matter, Antifa, and a collection of like-minded mentally unstable individuals. At its core, neo-racism, disguised as a vaguely defined "Black identity," is an African-American illness, a rapidly metastasizing cancer that kills and destroys the United States of America and the rest of the world. Their strategy is devoted to destructive goals almost in its entirety which are the foundation of Black culture. Its adherents' defense is that humanity in general and the African-American community in particular must be protected against the oppression of the White majority which is to be replaced by the rule of the colored people. What these race-baiters fail to answer is the question of how the creation of a neo-racist ideology would serve the interests of the United States of America, domestic tranquility, and the African-American community?

Instead, equipped with their one-sided justifications and civil unrest coupled with violence and mayhem have introduced political and economic instability that have further contributed to the radicalization of young African Americans in turn. In this manner, the neo-racist movement has been irreversibly infected with racial hatred against all non-Blacks. Therefore, "Black identity" is nothing but a negative identity. Ridiculously hysterical statements by celebrities, pop stars, athletes, and other semi-public figures have only amplified hatred and intolerance toward Whites, the United States of America, and past successes of the American people. Indeed, were it not for this assortment of American idiots, there would probably be no neo-racism in the United States of America and beyond. These American useful and useless idiots only perpetuate a Civil War-like situation domestically and cause damage to the United States of America's international reputation. This normalization of racist bigotry and hatred combined with the rejection of compromise, tolerance, and kindness should prevent any reasonable solutions to the impending civil war in the United States of America and beyond.

The neo-racism of these people is also based on their mythical and unreal narrative of eternal victimhood. Unless these victims attain total political and economic powers, there will be no peace in any society. Even White appeasement is rejected decisively. No for racial appropriation by non-Blacks and yes for neo-segregation. Collective guilt for the White majority but no collective guilt for Black people. Merit-based evaluation in education and professional life must be replaced with race-based privileges that go way beyond the objectives of the old affirmative action. All of these racially repugnant principles are the direct opposites of what American and Western cultures are about. The prophet Micah in the Bible warns, "O man, you have been told what is good and what it is that the Lord requires of you—only to do justice, to love kindness, and to walk humbly with your God." The neo-racists of today hate justice as well as kindness and love bottomless hatred. This is why they only know negativity and reject any positive sentiments and actions.

The Chinese-induced pandemic has contributed another destructive dimension to the general malaise of political and economic troubles around the globe. To add further insult to injury, the Biden administration has failed to comprehend the gravity of the situation. The neo-racist movement that the Democrats have diligently fueled and politically exploited to the hilt will have profound implications for generations to come. The horrors this movement already has triggered and certainly will continue to generate must be stopped immediately. The Biden administration must show zero tolerance toward neo-racism and all other forms of hatred toward anybody. Schools, beginning with kindergarten and continuing beyond graduate school, must teach love, kindness, tolerance, and the rejection of all forms of hatred as a defining sentiment of the people. Finally, these schools must educate young people that all human beings are worthy of respect and dignity in an environment free of oppression, intolerance, and hatred—a world rooted in freedom, democracy, and equal justice for all.

Therefore, from a very early age, Americans must be acquainted with the truth about Marxism, Fascism, and National Socialism. Most importantly, Marxism in any of its historical manifestations, has been a colossal failure. It did not work in the Soviet Union and Central and Eastern Europe. It has not worked in the People's Republic of China. It has abysmally failed in Central and South America. Similarly, Kwame Nkrumah and Jomo Kenyatta's "African Socialism" became a laughing stock, even in the former Soviet Union, Eastern Europe, and Mao's People's Republic of China. Equally, Fascism and National Socialism only brought worldwide tragedy to mankind. Thus, all of these extremely radical leftist ideologies proved their utter impracticality because of their inherent inhumanity. True, these ideologically obsessed idiots cannot be convinced by rational arguments. However, defending the truth about Marxism against their lies is mandatory for the sake of the future of the United States of America and its people.

Such truth is that to condemn Marxism, Leninism, Stalinism, Titoism, Maoism, Chavesism, etc., by and in itself is insufficient. Knowledgeable and sane people must elucidate to everybody that Marxism, which is based on unconditional class struggle and the absolute supremacy of the state by a self-selected despotic minority, is inherently Machiavellian and destructive. Moreover, the Marxist philosophy in general and its so-called "Historical Materialism" are blatantly unscientific, irredeemably impractical, and uselessly idealistic.

Having been imbued with the misguided German idealism of Georg Wilhelm Friedrich Hegel, Marx, as opposed to the propaganda lies of his followers, did not make Hegel's theoretical impracticality workable, but with his ideological rigidity, he rendered the latter's philosophy even more impractical. For Marx narrowed the ownership and means of production into being the only determinant of historical developments. Thus, he excluded everything else, such as technological progress, non-material developments, religion, the legal systems, constitutional constructs, etc.

Clearly, Marxism is not about "world happiness." Its real goals are the destruction of freedom, the total annihilation of individuality, the cultic and ruthless oppression of freedom of thought, and the establishment of the despotic rule of a small minority over the overwhelming majority. In these respects, Marxism is no better than Fascism and National Socialism. Revolution and ruthless class struggle are only means toward these immoral and inhuman goals. The dictatorship of the Communists, euphemistically labeled as "the dictatorship of the Proletariat", is nothing but the purest form of tyranny.

As such Communist/Socialist dictatorships have never known internal peace. What they had knowledge of and practiced with ruthless consistency has been oppression based on total fear. The most recent example of this thesis is the unfolding national protest movement in Cuba. The fact is that the Cuban people, regardless of their skin color, ethnicity, or professional background, are fed up with the Communist dictatorship that has systematically and institutionally been destroying the island nation politically, economically, and culturally as well as morally since early 1959.

While the Castro regime answered with police and military brutality, Black Lives Matter issued a statement on July 14, 2021, condemning the United States of America for the failure of the Castro dictatorship. The statement read thus, "Black Lives Matter condemns the U.S. federal government's inhumane treatment of Cubans, and urges it to immediately lift the economic embargo. […] This cruel and inhuman policy, instituted with the explicit intention of destabilizing the country and undermining Cubans' right to choose their own government, is at the heart of Cuba's current crisis."

These are blatant lies in their distorted description of Cuba's reality. Apparently, those Black Lives Matter supporters do not know that since Fidel Castro conquered Cuba, there have been no free elections in the country. Moreover, they appear to be criminally ignorant of the fact that the Castro regime has instituted the most "cruel and inhuman" policies in order to keep the Cuban people in virtual bondage to a ruthless dictatorship. Finally, even if the United States of America would have decided to assist the Cuban people economically, the Castro regime would have diverted any aid to itself.

Applying a self-serving "theoretical-ideological lens" to the current Cuban misery, this fallacious construct of Black Lives Matter best shows the true colors of this deranged movement. Accordingly, Black Lives Matter's willful ignorance demonstrates its poisonous modus operandi that shifts the burden of moral responsibility away from the real culprits and onto the persons or organizations inhabiting reality. This kind of Communist/Socialist manipulation that was the hallmark of the Soviet Union and is the main characteristic of the People's Republic of China must be clearly understood.

Since race and American racism cannot be left out, the statement continues, the U.S. "instigated suffering for the country's 11 million people—of which 4 million are Black and Brown." No comments are needed. However, the capacity to recognize Black Lives Matter for what it is—a bogus and dilettante nonentity—and resist it with all the power that decent people can marshal is the life-and-death situation for the American as well as Western civilizations. One should never forget the tragic lessons of history—the more tolerant and understanding societies have been to the hateful sociopaths in their ranks, the more vulnerable their members will be to the former's lies and manipulations in the long run.

4

The Present State of the Union

IN THE FALL of 2021, most Americans still live under the illusion that they exist in a free and democratic country. Yet, at least since the beginning of the Clinton presidency, the United States of America has been sliding toward the Stalinist-type dictatorship of a Leftist minority. President Clinton's attempt to socialize health care, young Bush's desire to introduce "compassionate conservatism," and Obama's all-out tactics to "fundamentally transform America" to a socialist nation were temporarily stopped by the Trump presidency.

However, throughout the entire Trump presidency, the United States of America was caught up in a permanent constitutional and political crisis. Beginning with Hillary Clinton's initial refusal to concede, continuing with the eternal big lie of the Russia Collusion, and culminating in two scandalous impeachments, the Democrat Party worked incessantly to destroy the domestic tranquility of the United States of America. Probably not by coincidence, these Democrat Party-made tactics coincided with an unusual exhibition and assertion of neo-racist radical rhetoric as well as extreme mayhem. The scale and impact of umpteenth acts of monstrous lawlessness committed by Black Lives Matter,

Antifa, the various platforms of Social Media, the written and electronic media, business conglomerates, and the Democrat Party across the country have been significant and appalling.

Preaching the false gospel of vulgar Marxism and the absurdly contradictory doctrine of Democratic Socialism, these organizations have transformed realities into shameful lies that have been designed to turn the American people into submissive idiots. Willful ignorance, fake epistemic ideas, and fraudulent promises to the American nation as well as the rest of the world have been the catastrophic flaws of these organizations' counterfeit realm.

This dystopian social engineering of the Democrat Party and its fellow travelers emphasizes the need for an authoritarian state, oppressive economic as well as financial controls, mandatory fear of an all-powerful bureaucracy, and the total loss of individuality. Historically, such an unreal and essentially artificial fiction of a state repeatedly ended in the authoritarian rulers irrational fear of their subjects and the concomitant efforts to corrupt the intellectual awareness of the people. Locked irremediably within these vicious circles of fear and lies, they have led individuals, societies, nations, and the world toward the inevitable universal suicide.

For these reasons, President Biden's fictional policy objectives enumerated in his mentally incoherent speech delivered to both Houses of Congress on April 27, 2021, are nothing but unconscionable political adventurism. Among the numerous demented gems of this mentally ill individual, the most idiotic was the following statement, "We the people are the government." To start with, in a normal democracy, the majority governs, and the minority forms a loyal opposition. The phrase "We the People" does not equate the government with the people. Governments are the results of elections. Ideally, they do represent all of the people.

In practice, they represent a majority and should also govern for the benefit of the minority. The range of opposition to the majority could vary from election to election, thus equating his administration with the people is a lie because it does not reflect reality. As Bryon York wrote in his insightful daily memo on May 3, 2021, President Biden has no mandate from the American people "to remake America." Moreover, President Biden's assertion is also unconstitutional. Clearly, his statement only widens the divisions within the country. Finally, his claim represents a continuing source of instability in the already fragmented climate of politics and culture across the nation.

Had President Biden had the mental capacity to comprehend the present state of the Union, he should have called for the nation to return to the core and humanistic principles and values of its founding documents. Democracy cannot exist in a country where truth, honesty, trust, and a realistic vision of the future is absent. From day one as president, he has instead embraced the lies, coverups, and intellectual as well as material frauds within his party and their supporting organizations. He has based decisions on his and his party's political and personal gains. He loudly claimed to support healing and unity throughout his shadow campaign from his basement, but once in office, he has executed countless U-turns, putting his support behind exactly the opposite of what he forcefully criticized and even demonized previously. Cynically, he and his fellow travelers have created more divisions, fragmentations, and enmities than he inherited from his predecessors.

At the beginning of his "healing" and "uniting" speech, President Biden stated that he "inherited a nation in crisis" and defined America as a "house on fire." Not able to resist an unbecoming dig at his predecessor, he did not say who caused the crisis and who lit America on fire. Continuing in the same pathological vein, he declared, "Now, after 100 days, I can report to the nation—America is on the move again." In reality, America is on the move in the wrong direction, both domestically as well as internationally.

Faithful to his lying narrative, he continued, "America is rising anew. Choosing hope over fear. Truth over lies. Light over darkness. After 100 days of rescue and renewal, America is ready to take off. We are working again. Dreaming again. Discovering again. Leading the world again." Lies upon lies. Either America is in a crisis and on fire, or it rises? Based on his avalanche of executive orders, the country is not ready to take off. America under his administration is not leading anything except chaos and anarchy across the globe.

Similarly, America is not working normally. Ubiquitous violence, mayhem, and the accompanying destruction, uncontrolled illegal immigration with gang members and organized crime from Central and South America, and terrorists from all over the world will never help America work again as before. As a result, increasing numbers of Americans are living in fear and not in hope. Finally, with all of these lies, how can he claim that he has chosen truth over lies? In reality, his speech again proved he is a liar par excellence and a mentally handicapped fraud.

This verdict was proven again by his next statement, "We won't ignore what our own intelligence agencies have determined—the most lethal terrorist threat to the homeland today is from White supremacist's terrorism." To add insult to injury, he mused over the work that must be done "to rebuild trust between law enforcement and the people they serve, to root out systematic racism in our criminal justice system." These combined sentences make no sense at all.

Calling the majority's natural reactions to the uncontrolled violence, mayhem, and destruction of Black Lives Matter, Antifa, and the mob "White supremacist terrorism" is nothing but naked abuse of the English language and the pathological ignorance of the realities on the ground. Truth over lies? No. Lies over truths!

His suggestion "to rebuild trust between law enforcement and the people" is also false. The overwhelming majority of Americans are law abiding and trust the uniform. The overwhelming majority of police forces are well trained and very professional. The mostly Black violence cannot be stopped by "rooting out systematic racism in our criminal justice system." Black criminals do not want to compromise. They demand absolute impunity for their crimes. They want total submission by the overwhelming majority to their destructive actions. Thus, instead of promoting unity on the national scale, President Biden deepened the schism between the races in America. Again, instead of a bright future full of truth and hope, President Biden is spreading lies that surely will generate untold tragedies and catastrophes not seen before in American history.

Proving the reality of President Biden's mental confusion and his unending cries of America allegedly being "systematically racist," he recently stated, "I don't think the American people are racist." Of course, the question arises in any normal person— how can America be racist if its people are not? Moreover, can a country that twice elected a Black president be systematically and institutionally racist? As Liz Peek pointed out in her opinion, Whites are not even the most prosperous group as measured by median household income. "Indeed, it is Indian Americans who earn the highest income by far in the U.S. at more than $119,000, followed by Taiwanese Americans, Filipino Americans, and Chinese Americans. White Americans are only the ninth most prosperous group, with median incomes just shy of $66,000."

The fact that Black Americans rank last with median average income of $41,500 only proves that skin color is not the driving force behind the native-born Black problems. To wit, Black immigrants earn on the average of one-third more than members of the previous group. Even his deputy, Vice President Kamala Harris had to admit on ABC News that "I don't think America is a racist country, but we also do have to speak the truth about the history of racism in our country and its existence today."

But back to President Biden's speech. After the toxic and hateful rant about American racism came the Marxian dictum of transferring wealth from the rich to the poor in its most vulgar manifestation. Slavishly adhering to Barack Obama's primitive demand that the wealthy must "pay their fair share," this demented current occupant of the White House intoned, "It's time for corporate America and the wealthiest 1% of Americans to pay their fair share. Just pay their fair share."

This idiotic claim begs the questions such as who belongs to the 1%? Who determines the boundaries? What is a "fair share"? Who will define it? Then came the creme on his spoiled apple pie. Stating that his tax reforms are aimed at "reward(ing) work, not wealth" and will only affect "three tenths of 1% of all Americans," President Biden again used revolting lies to justify his party's destruction of the middle class, the hard-working small business owners, and the entire economy. The good news, however, is that President Biden's tax proposals will be dead on arrival in both Houses of Congress. Beginning with his proposed increases in capital gains taxes to raising the corporate taxes, Democrats will not be ready to commit political suicide en masse.

In closing, he turned to the events on January 6, 2021. Predictably, he called the storming of the Capitol "the worst attack on our democracy since the Civil War." In addition to ignoring many previous events in American history, most eminently September 11, 2001, President Biden again divided the nation into his party's partisans and the American people who disagree with them. His speech merely proved a single truth— for President Biden, lies are realities. For this reason alone, he is not a normal person. To build a delusional world for himself makes him a useful idiot in the hands of the very extremist wing of the Democrat Party. Indeed, he is not the real president. He is a pawn in the ruthless powerplay of Vice President Kamala Harris, members of his "diverse" cabinet, and the neo-racist mob against the United States of America.

The Republican answer was delivered by South Carolina Senator Tim Scott. The editorial Board of *The New York Post* started its editorial on April 19, 2021, with the following sentence, "Kudos to Sen. Tim Scott for his slam-dunk response to President Joe Biden's speech Wednesday night, calling out the president's hypocrisy and demanding he start walking the 'unity' walk." Then the editorial continued, "And he did it with some killer lines, noting that 'a president who promised to bring us together' is 'pushing agendas that tear us apart' and scoffing of the refusal to negotiate Biden's $2.3 trillion infrastructure plan that Democrats 'won't even build bridges to build bridges.' But Sen. Scott was most effective on 'Biden's talk of systematic racism.'"

After recounting his experience with discrimination, he said, "America is not a racist country. It's backwards to fight discrimination with different discrimination." Turning to Georgia's voting reform the Senator said, "Race is not a political weapon to sell every issue the way one side wants."

In his excellent speech, Senator Scott also rejected Wokeism in the strongest terms and the anti-Americanism of the Democrat Party, the media, and the mob. He reaffirmed the importance of the rule of law and its enforcement by the police. He exposed the lies and dishonesty of Biden's speech. None other than Democrat Congressman Jim Clyburn of South Carolina, the House Majority Whip, agreed with Senator Tim Scott.

First, he agreed with Senator Scott that America is not a racist country, saying, "I don't think a racist country would have elected Barack Obama as president or Kamala Harris as vice president." The next day, according to Fox News, Congressman Clyburn said that America is "not about being perfect, but when you see a fault, repair it. We got a fault today in our law enforcement. Let's repair it. There's a fault today with 47 states now coming out with these voter suppression laws. Come on, United States of America, let's repair it." Then he quoted Alexis de Tocqueville's well-known description of America in 1835, "America is not great because it is more enlightened than any other nation but rather because it has always been able to repair its faults." Fair enough.

Naturally, the imminent merchant of race baiting and the spiritual anti-American terrorist Al Sharpton also jumped into the anti-Scott ring, stating, "I watched, the other night, the president make his first address to the joint session of Congress. And then I watched the rebuttal by the senator from South Carolina on April 21. Seems something awkward to me, where a White president talked about White supremacy and a Black senator said [...] America is not racist. Seemed a little strange to me." Following these lies, Al Sharpton descended into the depths of irrationality, "Now, everybody in America is not racist. But are you talking about whether the practice of America's racist or the people because the practice of America was built on racism." What a useless idiot!

For his honest evaluation of President Biden's speech and what needs to be done, Senator Scott has earned the vehemently racist abuse and disparagement of the neo racist horde. The mildest form of these racist invectives was "Uncle Tim." MSNBC host Tiffany Cross accused Senator Scott of being "thirsty for White approval." Again on MSNBC, a panel of Marxist university professors declared the use of the racial slur "Uncle Tim" to characterize Senator Scott an ignoramus who "doesn't know what racism is."

Proving the idiocy of some university professors, Christina Geer asserted, "I mean, let's be clear, looking at Tim Scott's response, we know that he's carrying the water, not just for the Republican Party and his two other Black colleagues, but he did so under the Trump administration, and that's where the lack of respect comes from." She then went on to repeat the lie about the Republican Party's sole responsibility for the past and present conditions in the Black community.

Senator Scott responded to these "stunning" personal assaults by saying that it was shocking to hear intolerance coming from those who say they want to end discrimination, and that those attacking him were doubling down on the concept of liberal oppression. Taking a global view, the Senator stated, "Their America and my America aren't the same America if in fact they think that discriminating is the fastest way to end discrimination." Finally, he concluded, "Racism and discrimination—it's still real, but it is being pushed further and further into a smaller corner in our nation. That's great news that we should celebrate. If you want to be an American, the door is wide open. The front door, by the way, is wide open to come in and add value to who we are, not be part of destructive conversations that belittle individuals."

Clearly, it is not a time to discuss who is more or less racist, to accuse individuals irresponsibly and without any real evidence, or to engage in false rhetoric concerning the COVID-19 pandemic. These are important matters that must be addressed and solved, yet addressing these issues in a biased way and laced with lies does not contribute to satisfactory solutions. If "We the People" do not share basic values and a common language, not a single problem can be solved in America. As Senator Scott said, we must calmly re-examine who we really are, what really matters to us, what our governing principles are, and why they are of primary importance to both the individual as well as the nation as a whole. Only after that's done can the United States of America begin the healing process within an alarmingly fractured society.

However, in order to achieve such a state of affairs, public figures on both sides of the aisle must love America as well as its inhabitants unconditionally and regardless of their differing political affiliations. Conversely, the people's lack of belief in the unbiased sincerity of their representatives will surely result in the complete miscarriage of the intended policies and in painful personal tragedies. Thus, to avoid the ubiquitous confusion of lies, misinformation, and innuendos, the American people must use common sense and what the Romans already defined as "reductio ad absurdum."

According to this basic principle of logic, if the conclusion obtained from the prerequisite contradicts reality, the prerequisite must be rejected as untrue. Naturally, one cannot totally exclude emotions. However, emotions should not overwhelm intellect. This way, information, regardless of its sources, must represent light and not darkness of human decisions.

Let's hark back again to President Biden's often quoted speech in which he intoned, "My whole soul is in [...] bringing America together, uniting our people, and uniting our nation [...] uniting to fight the common foes we face: anger, resentment, hatred, extremism, lawlessness, violence, disease, joblessness, hopelessness." These are all noble endeavors. However, he first should look into the mirror and after that act according to his newly discovered kindness and wisdom.

Regrettably, however, President Biden's vision of America is an alarmingly narrow one. More importantly, it is in direct conflict with the expectations of the majority of Americans. While his ideology attempts to make Americans feel good, it will politically, economically, and intellectually prove to be an unmitigated disaster. His political alliances of temporary conveniences will quickly disintegrate and leave him and his party in a classic quagmire. Driven by his extremist ideology, his political and economic tactics will lead to incompetent overreaching and ruinous political as well as economic conditions. Thus, instead of restoring America's greatness, President Biden's four years will be remembered as a precipitous decline in the United States of America's global positions.

Every American should stop, pause, and ask him or herself why in the economically most prosperous and technologically advanced country, a little more than one-tenth of the population exists below the poverty line. The now much maligned Founding Fathers had a vision of a Republic that rejected tyranny, oppression by a minority, and exploitation. Positively, their vision embraced freedom, democracy, and creativity.

They bequeathed upon future generations a country of Judeo-Christian morality, a justice system independent of political and biased emotional influences, and the opportunity of social equality. A country full of kindness, compassion, and caring. A country that welcomed everybody who came to be a productive part of the noblest experiment in human history. A country that could have been called home by all kinds of refugees. A country in which everybody can be free and prosper regardless of their country of origin, color of their skin, or ethnic affiliation. Assimilation, not divergence, was the founding ideal behind the United States of America's creation and its raison d'état.

For these reasons, that kind of poverty rate is morally unacceptable. This or any other poverty rate condemns successive generations to an uncertain and possibly grim future. Presently, the anti-American demagogues use these unfortunate young people to forge an army that is the enemy from within. Moreover, these demagogues have forged a political weapon out of these less fortunate to indoctrinate the majority with their pathological lies and hatred. The ultimate objective of Black Lives Matter, Antifa, and the extremist wing of the Democrat Party are absolutely determined to overthrow America's political, socio-economic, and moral foundations which is far more deadly than the People's Republic of China, the Russian Federation, or any other external enemies of our country.

Yet, the most discouraging phenomenon of the so-called "war on poverty" has been that both Democrats and Republicans have been satisfied with mindlessly throwing money at the problems while lacking any thoughtful and long-term strategy on how to really eradicate poverty. Here, the charges of bias and discrimination are partially warranted, albeit not to the extent that the race-baiting demagogues claim. The country that has prided itself of being a melting pot has discriminated against certain ethnic groups in housing, lending, recruiting, and employment. Unfortunately, the well-intentioned but misguided affirmative action has not helped to remedy the situation either.

In this respect, allow me a personal experience. In 1979, I received a call from a friend in the White House. He informed me that a high position in one of the federal intelligence agencies became vacant. The job required thorough knowledge of the Soviet Union and its Eastern European holdings. In addition, knowledge of Russian and preferably other languages spoken in the region was also a must. Although I had no intention to leave my position with Congress, I was interviewed for the job. A week later, the same friend informed me that the position is subject to affirmative action and therefore only a Black person would be accepted. To my knowledge, the job was never filled because of the dearth of qualified candidates.

For these political errors, the consequences have been most visible in education. While America has rightly been proud of and boasted about its excellent universities, resourcefulness, and creativity, children in poverty have been lagging behind their contemporaries in educational ambitions and achievements. Regrettably, because of all this, America's greater than 300 million population is neither economically satisfactory nor socially unified. This situation, in turn, has led to political polarization and the accompanying disagreements about the basic principles upon which the United States of America rests. The 2020 election provided enough convincing evidence that the country and its people are disgruntled with the existing political atmosphere to a dangerous degree.

Because of the dearth of bipartisanship in Congress, there is little hope that a comprehensive strategy to at least reduce indoctrination and intellectual poverty in education could be agreed upon between Democrats and Republicans. However, only such a bipartisan bill would have a chance to alleviate the hopeless situation of future generations of the poor and thus facilitate the gradual eradication of entrenched poverty.

Still, the Biden administration has pushed for the irredeemably biased and untrue Critical Race Theory to be taught in K-12 public and charter schools. Presently, Idaho, Oklahoma, and Tennessee have already passed legislation to ban this racist ideological garbage from being disseminated by their teachers. Commendably, many other states are considering similar measures to block the teaching of Critical Race Theory instruction and material which also includes 1619 Project material, more race-baiting ideological filth promoted by the Biden administration.

Meanwhile, on average, one-third of K-12 public school students cannot read properly, and a quarter of high school graduates must take remedial courses to qualify for college-level studies. These ominous numbers indicate that federal, state, local, and school officials care more about Soviet-style indoctrination than about teaching academically worthwhile and professionally productive subjects.

However, the most critical situation for future progress of the entire nation is the abysmal condition of education, or more precisely indoctrination, at the college and graduate-school levels. According to Michael Poliakoff, the survival of academic freedom in higher education is at stake. In his article published under the title "Campus Ideology's Slippery Slope" by *Newsweek* on May 6, 2021, he stated, "A civil and unprejudiced campus is a priority for any academic community that is true to its purpose. But when a community of scholars and teachers, especially a famous and influential one, trades time-honored principles of free inquiry for reflexive and enforced social theories, it damages the broader social fabric." Pointing to Cornell University, he asserts that "Cornell University is, at the moment, ground zero in this ideological battle, though it is not alone in considering whether to require training on race, diversity, and equity. Official working groups at Cornell recently proffered proposals to address such issues as settler colonialism, White privilege, structural racism, injustice, and bias. Their 'Educational Requirements for Anti-Racist, Just, and Equitable Futures' is aggressive and expansive."

As Poliakoff alluded to, the ghosts of Soviet educational norms are all over this intellectually worthless pamphlet. Again, two personal experiences. I was in the final semester of my third year at the university in Hungary when I gave a speech about the so-called Six Day War between Israel and the five Arab states. During my speech, I mentioned a report by Voice of America in which the role of the Soviet Union was discussed. An assistant professor who was present at my speech reported my comments to the dean of the faculty. I had to apologize publicly and promise that I would not listen again to "hostile radio stations," particularly those of American and British origin.

Another event occurred just prior to my graduation. I wrote an essay that was nominated as worthy of a national scientific prize. Before I was scheduled to speak at the University of Debrecen, one of my professors called me into his office and ordered me to omit a passage critical of Soviet and Hungarian criminal jurisprudence from my presentation. I did not comply. Again, I was hauled before the dean of the faculty and punished by taking away my gold medal for the most excellent presentation.

The echoes of Soviet-style indoctrination could be heard once again in the following list of demands, quoted by Michael Poliakoff in his article, "We can and must honor academic freedom and disciplinary authority without allowing such principles to serve as mechanisms for perpetuating structural racism." In order to prevent such a gross violation of social justice and equity, Cornell faculty, graduate students, and staff declared that Cornell "remains a site of entrenched racial disparities" that must change, because it is "complicit, in countless ways, in the reproduction of White supremacy." What follows is a list, better defined as authoritarian demands, to "embed decolonized readings in every possible course at Cornell" and to "abolish color-blind recruitment policies and practices [...] and replace them with intentionally anti-racist policies and practices." In plain English, abolish the merit-based recruitment and replace it with racist favoritism. Translated to the Soviet vocabulary, a stupid Communist is preferable to a smart outsider.

Tragically, the other so-called top universities are not far behind. Similar to Poliakoff's article, countless other writings have pointed out the destructive demagoguery of these neo-racist warriors, especially Victor Davis Hanson of the Hoover Institution who has so poignantly illustrated the intolerable state of affairs in higher education in many articles and opinions. In one of his latest commentaries in the *DailySignal* with the title "Are Americans Becoming Sovietized?", he listed it as the first symptom of the "nihilist Soviet system of lies and hypocrisies" ideological indoctrination.

As he opined, "A job in the bureaucracy or a military assignment hinged not so much on merit, expertise, or past achievement. What mattered was loud enthusiasm for the Soviet system." Spot on! Further down he said, "The Soviet education system sought not to enlighten but to indoctrinate young minds in proper government approved thoughts." In conclusion, he stated, "The Soviets mastered Trotskyization or the rewriting and airbrushing away of history to fabricate present reality." Absolutely true! The tragedy is, however, that the Soviet Union is dead and the Russian President has repudiated the Soviet era in general as well as Lenin, Stalin, and all of the other dead icons of the debunked Soviet history. Meanwhile, an assorted horde of idiots, masquerading as the geniuses of America, are embracing a system of government that failed everywhere.

More importantly, the practical consequences of the Democrat Party's race baiting in education through monstrous lies about American history has been a dramatic increase in hate crimes committed mostly by Blacks against Asians and Jews across the United States of America. From the West Coast to the East Coast, hate crimes by unemployed and marauding Black youth have multiplied alarmingly. Democrat-governed California, Oregon, and Washington have experienced a stupendous rise in violent hate crimes against Whites, Asians, Hispanics, and Jews.

In New York City alone where one of those incompetent Democrat idiots is the mayor, hate crimes have seen a 73% rise in a single year against Asians and Jews. In 2021, according to the New York Police Department's Hate Crime Task Force, it was revealed that in the first five months of 2021, 180 hate crimes were committed against these two groups. Most of those hate crimes have been violent and sustained. Chicago, another big city governed by Democrats, has also seen a dramatic increase in hate crimes, mostly against Asian inhabitants. The conclusion that these two groups have been singled out because of their successes in education and work are not farfetched.

Clearly, attempts at dumbing down education to the lowest level only results in ubiquitous jealousy, hatred, and violence. The Marxist-Maoist Critical Race Theory exclusively teaches hatred by indoctrination. It has been founded on a chain of lies that consist of fallacious constructions of reality. If allowed to take root in the school systems, it will destroy education and render the United States of America a third-rate country.

Therefore, it is hopefully obvious that it must be fought with all of the tools available to parents, educators, and public figures. An encouraging example of standing up to this deliberately evil understanding of reality is the Dallas suburb of Southlake. Recently, parents of various ethnicities, faiths, and political persuasions voted out the entire anti-American schoolboard and replaced them with members who committed themselves to resisting Marxist-Maoist indoctrination of their children. The votes against the former members were overwhelming. More than 70% of the attendees voted for a completely new school-board in Southlake.

More recently, Loudoun County, Virginia, parents have taken the lead against Critical Race Theory. As the *Washington Examiner* reported on May 28, 2021, angry parents have launched a petition to recall several members of the schoolboard who they deem responsible for injecting CRT into the county's school curriculum. As one mother put it, "Critical Race Theory is racist; it is abusive; it discriminates against one's color."

To wit, Critical Race Theory has been further radicalized by the neo-resegregation ideology of many Black students. Declaring that White students are not welcome among Blacks student because "this is a space for people of color, so just be really cognizant of the space you're taking up because it does make us [people of color] uncomfortable when we see too many White people in here" is an attempt to return to the past that Blacks have condemned as "systematic and institutionalized racism." The irrationality and dictatorial hypocrisy of the neo-re-segregation movement is again self-evident. Its one-sidedness, self-defeatism, and unsustainability should be clear to every sane person. Yet, Democrat Party politicians of all colors and persuasions have enthusiastically embraced and promoted this ideology of discombobulated nonsense.

Hand in hand with this fake intellectual cult mentality by a miniscule minority of race-obsessed idiots, President Biden has decided to pursue economic policies that will move America toward a totalitarian Marxist-Maoist open-border country. *The New York Times*, in its childish enthusiasm, recently headlined Biden's call for "Big Government" as the proper response to a "Nation Tested by Crisis." True to its devious abuse of the English language, the paper hailed the largest expansion of the federal government's taxing, spending, and bureaucratic powers as the only possible remedy for revitalizing the pandemic-devastated economy. With a $6 trillion proposed spending binge, the Biden administration and the Democrat-controlled Congress have decided to dramatically reverse Bill Clinton's proclamation that "the era of big government is over."

Monies to cover this orgy of the federal government's drunken-sailor spending will naturally have to come from astronomical personal, business, and corporate taxes. If adopted, the United States of America will have the dubious honor of being the most severely taxed country among the industrialized states. More importantly, no economist in the world would even be able to predict for sure whether these enormous tax increases would cover the spending in all of these fancily named plans. With small businesses being suffocated by higher hourly rate salaries and with members of the middle class struggling to maintain their standard of living, the Biden Administration and the Democrat Party are leading the United States of America toward the deepest abyss of national bankruptcy.

This ominous prediction is echoed by K.S. Bruce's insightful commentary *Joe Biden, Economy Killer*. Listing inflation, federal deficits, high taxes, incentives for workers to stay home, and incentives to avoid investment, he concludes that "these elements create the perfect brew for a Lyndon Johnson-style stagflation." He predicts that "if Biden and the Democrats so quickly wreck the good economic path they were given, it will be one of the worst examples of government malpractice in U.S. economic history."

K.S. Bruce also sees the many signs of the coming great inflation. Again, he goes back to Lyndon Johnson's Great Society spending. Quoting Michael Bryan of the Federal Reserve Bank of Atlanta, "In 1964, inflation measured little more than 1 percent per year. It had been in this vicinity for the preceding six years. Inflation began ratcheting upward in the mid-1960s and reached more than 14 percent in 1980. [...] The Great Inflation was the defining macroeconomic event of the second half of the twentieth century." K.S. Bruce warns that the disaster of Biden's plan "after inflation and slow growth will be when the rising interest rates created by the inflation cause the government's own interest rates and cost of borrowing to rise." In conclusion, he says, "Whichever Democrat casts the 50th vote to throw the U.S. economy off the precipice will earn their own piece of economic immortality."

On its May 28, 2021, editorial, the Editorial Board of Issues & Insights called President Biden's proposed budget "mammoth." Its total spending will be $6 trillion in 2022 with a deficit of $1.8 trillion. According to the editorial, it is a 36 percent rise above the pre-pandemic spending of $4.4 trillion in 2019. The editorial cites the Congressional Budget Office's estimate showing that President Biden's spending plan would add $22 trillion to the existing deficit. Again, according to the editorial, that translates into a massive unsustainable increase in publicly held federal debt from an estimated $22.6 trillion this year to just under $43 trillion in 2031. As a useful comparison, the editorial noted that it took the U.S. more than 210 years to reach $5 trillion in total federal debt. In the 22 years since then, we've added 3.6 times that amount.

Combined with such gigantic political incompetence and professional stupidity has been President Biden's open-border policy. The ultimate purpose of creating deliberate confusion in the asylum policies of the federal government is power. This deliberately created chaos and anarchy by the Democrat Party serves the purpose of politically favoring those who are ready to accept the pseudo-humanitarian justification of inherent refugees. Accordingly, everybody who leaves his country of domicile must be a refugee. However, the definition of "refugee" has been firmly anchored in the 1951 Refugee Convention and its 1967 Protocol that were signed and ratified by the U.S. Senate. Therefore, both multilateral agreements are part of the American domestic law and binding on the federal government.

Article 1 of the Convention defines a "refugee" as a person who is outside his or her country of nationality or habitual residence, has a well-founded fear of persecution because of his race, religion, nationality, membership in a particular social group, or political opinion and is unable or unwilling to avail himself of the protection of that country, or not having a nationality and being outside the country of his former habitual residence as a result of such events is unable or owing to such fear unwilling to return to it.

The overwhelming majority of persons flooding the southern border are not refugees. They are individuals trying to enter the U.S. illegally because of existential and not political reasons. Therefore, they are not qualified for asylum. They are illegal immigrants, plain and simple. This is the reality. This is the truth. President Biden and the Democrat Party have created a double standard. A refugee is every illegal immigrant whom they declare to be a legal asylum seeker. Clearly, this decision is political and has nothing to do with legal reasoning. The thus illegally created double standard favors the Democrat Party and disfavors those who insist on adherence to the rule of law. By this discombobulated logic, the illegal immigrant does not have to prove his or her eligibility for asylum under the law, but the federal government must apply its self-serving double standard to ascertain that an illegal immigrant is actually a lawful refugee. In this manner, breaking the law by entering American territory illegally is an act that cannot be punished, due to the capricious character of the Biden administration.

These measures already taken by the Biden administration also represent the crassest instances of anti-law enforcement and pro-criminal deeds perpetrated by any administration throughout history. They blatantly ignore national security and federal as well as state laws. They protect international criminal organizations that are enjoying impunity to victimize Americans. Clearly, it is a most serious threat for the United States of America.

Such behavior by the government is qualified as authoritarian. Clearly, the Biden Administration and the Democrat Party granted itself the extra-judicial power to politically redefine the term "refugee" in contravention of the law. Under these circumstances, insistence upon the rule of law is proof of immorality, inhumanity, and even criminal attitude by any opponent of this illegal and amoral double standard. Taking and falsely occupying the imaginary high moral ground of pseudo-humanism, these sham champions of obvious lies and distortions intend to demoralize everybody who dares to shed light on their disgraceful falsifications of language and blatant disregard of the law.

As such, attempting to monopolize falsehoods and deceptions, President Biden and his fellow Democrats pretend to be normal while they are abnormal, and they accuse the normal majority of being out of line with the natural progress of history. The danger for America is that President Biden, with his distorted logic, can no longer perceive reality, and as a result, he is definitively trapped in his self-created vicious circle of lies and deceptions. With this sick and subverted thinking and mentality that conceives reality as illusion and illusion as reality, he and the United States of America with him jointly exist in the total darkness of President Biden's mental asylum.

5

The Coming Backlash

THE PRESENTLY ONGOING anti-American hate campaign against the overwhelming majority of the citizenry by a miniscule portion of the Black minority has been rooted in the long-simmering emotional jealousy of the latter against the more accomplished members of the nation. This unjustified and exclusively destructive feeling has triggered calls for violent revenge in the form of anarchistic actions to destroy the existing conditions in society and replace them with the rule of these emotionally scarred misfits with psychopathic tribal mentalities.

Today, just when the extent of the scope and the magnitude of the hypocritical as well as the destructively violent nature of Black Lives Matter, Antifa, and like-minded hordes are fully realized, the Biden Administration has been undertaking the most inhumane and evidently most counterproductive policies to further divide the United States of America. Contrary to the opinions of the intellectually misguided and politically biased media, appeasing these psychopaths will certainly lead to more chaos and anarchy in politics, result in suffocating the pandemic-devastated economy, and raise the specter of more control by an authoritarian federal government across the Union.

This unrelenting onslaught on the domestic peace and stability of the nation has also been directed against the most precious asset of America—its boundless creativity. This unbounded creativity has been the result of the liberties and freedoms that have been firmly anchored by the Founding Fathers in the Declaration of Independence and the Constitution with all of its amendments. Human creativity has been the engine of America's successes throughout history. In 2021, at the dawn of the Fourth Industrial Revolution, also called the Coming Age of Artificial Intelligence, nations and cultures that allow human creativity to flourish without undue political control will perform humanly, economically, and financially much better than those nations who will lack the wherewithal to raise their threshold of creative freedoms.

For these reasons, exhausting the human resources of the United States of America in endlessly contrived debates about unreal problems that do not exist, such as 'White supremacy" and "systematic and institutionalized racism" would only condemn the nation to decades of stagnation or even underperformance in sciences, domestic progress, international standing, and goodwill. The president, leaders of the Democrat Party, and the majority of journalists have insisted their main objective is to defeat those who oppose the deliberate destruction of the country. Exclusively focusing and overemphasizing mostly imaginary problems is only intended to paralyze and destroy the nation.

Therefore, the United States of America must overhaul the foundations of its education, economic, and financial systems. Only this way will the United States of America be considered by the rest of the world to be the undisputed leader and most valued strategic partner for other states. Reforms and not psychopathic delusions by an emotionally excitable mob with little or no genuine education will bring the American ideal of ubiquitous freedom to enduring triumph. Such a paradigm switch from the multitude of fake problems that have been pushed by a miniscule minority and weaponized by the Obama and Biden Democrats to "America the solution" is essential for the survival as well as the unbroken development of the American ideal.

Policies by the Biden administration of being victims of "White supremacy" and the champions of all victimized minorities across the globe simultaneously have only contributed to the ubiquitous chaos and confusion in the world. No great power such as the United States of America can sustain its number one ranking by merely instilling global fear of impending catastrophes, be it the unscientific global warming, nuclear catastrophes, or equally idiotic universal identity politics. Instead of practicing political healing and unifying the nation to face major domestic and international challenges, President Biden and the Democrat Party have been busy unilaterally altering the organization of society. As such, they are as threatening of the future for the nation as the thugs of Black Lives Matter, Antifa, and all like-minded domestic-terrorist hordes.

Patriotism versus tribalism must be taught in every kindergarten and in every school as scientifically proven truth over the pathological lies of racism as well as the unscientific tribalism of identity politics. Patriotism, defined as an honest implementation of the democratic principles firmly embedded in the Constitution which have historically embodied the hopes and aspirations of all Americans, must remain the educational foundation of the uniquely American democracy.

Conversely, race-based tribalism that only teaches hatred toward everyone who does not belong to a certain race must be decisively rejected as fatally destructive and ideological garbage. It is as far away from real patriotism and democracy as the eponymous tyranny of the tribal chiefs and the despotism of the present authoritarian rulers across the African continent. Moreover, Black Lives Matter and Antifa's race-based tribalism propagates a kind of vulgar Socialism and Communism that absolutely lacks any morality, honesty, or love for humanity. Finally, these extreme anarchist groups call upon everybody to trample on the constitution as though it were just a piece of worthless paper.

To wit, their political masters in the Democrat Party want to transform elections into miserable farces and pack the Supreme Court with their ideologically subservient political marionettes. Since the disastrous presidency of Barack Obama, they have done their level best to discredit the United States of America and its democracy. They have attempted to suppress any opposition by intimidation, violence, and outright terror. Adding pathological insult to political injury, they also have tried to replace "We the People" with the personal dictatorship of a miniscule minority.

As a result, nobody is safe in the United States of America. Nobody, when he or she goes to bed at night, knows what awaits him or her when the new day breaks. The righteous and the innocent are presumed guilty because of their skin, race, or gender, while the perpetrators of crimes are declared victims of discrimination and enjoy impunity which is exactly the way Hitler's Germany and Stalin's Soviet Union functioned, to the horror of mankind.

Hiding behind the false slogans of war against racism, they intend to instill terror in the hearts and minds of the "enemies of the people." By putting political hacks with no real education and experience in responsible government positions, they have corrupted the impartial functioning of every federal and state organization.

Declaring their pathological lies to be infallible truths, they have attempted to turn their abuse of intellectual idiocies and authoritarian distortions of their powers in the name of a future utopian happiness into a ubiquitous psychopathic herd mentality. By trying to annihilate the glorious past of the United States of America, they are making life unbearable for the American people.

In fact, the failures of violently building utopias were illustrated by Edmund Burke in his *Reflections on the Revolution in*

France, Andre Paul Guillaume Gide's reports in his *Return from the Soviet Union*, and *The German Dictatorship* by Karl Dietrich Bracher, who all tried to redefine society at large as well as truth, justice, and equality. Ignoring realities, these three so-called revolutions had no second thoughts about running roughshod over history, especially the past, culture, institutions, and moral principles of a nation. Their common justification for all of their monstrous horrors was their claim of wanting to usher in a future of absolute egalitarianism.

Their successors, such as Mao Zedong, Kim Il Sung, Fidel Castro, Pol Pot, Hugo Chavez, Kim Jong Il, Kim Jong Un, and Robert Mugabe and his fellow African despots, have all professed to labor for the wholesome benefits of their peoples' future, while in reality, they have rendered their subjects more primitive, idiotical, and "atavistic," to quote Marxist literature. According to *Forbes News*, while technological developments are on the rise, IQ rates are on decline across the globe. Surveying studies from Europe, Asia, Africa, and the United States of America, the Forbes article of April 29, 2020, concluded that studies conducted in Denmark, Norway, and the United Kingdom "are seeing a noticeable slowing—and even reversal—of IQ."

Quoting a 2018 *Science Alert* article by Peter Dockrill, "An analysis of some 730,000 IQ test results by researchers from the Ragnar Frisch Centre for Economic Research in Norway reveals the Flynn effect hit its peak for people born during the mid-1970s and has declined ever since." Similar studies in other European countries and the United States of America have demonstrated the same trend in IQ scores. Although most of the studies point to environmental causes, in reality, the politicization of education by one-sided indoctrination to the detriment of unbiased education render the children, from a very early age, incapable of developing independent judgment on their surroundings, life in general, and their professions.

The best illustration of most teachers' mentality in the United States of America was a recent interview on Martha McCallum's show *The Story* on Fox News with the President of American Federation of Teachers (AFT) Randi Weingarten. McCallum questioned Weingarten's agenda to propagate the 1619 Project in public schools as a definite and reliable history of the founding of America as well as its claim that "the reason for the revolution and the colonization was because people wanted to preserve slavery." Weinberger, a self-described "history and social studies teacher" replied, "From everything I can see and understand from the data that I see, 1619 was the year that the first slave boat came from Africa to the United States. So that's a point in history that I think we should teach." Maybe? But mixing up the arrival of a boat full of illiterate poor souls with the establishment of the United States of America by the highly educated and very intelligent Founding Fathers is fraud by any intellectual standard.

Not content with showing her ideological bias, Ms. Weingarten voiced her belief that "the country was founded on the basis of wanting to preserve slavery." Her narrow-mindedness and even glaring stupidity do not require further comments. Martha McCallum, however, remarked, "If you raise children in this country believing that it's a bad country that was founded in wanting to preserve slavery [...] then we've got a problem in our school system." In her continued rebuttal, Ms. McCallum went on to state, "That is not true. In fact, scholars say there's no evidence that colonists were motivated by that in coming to the United States, so it would be wrong as a historian to want to teach them something that is not true, because that is the basis that sets up all of these other tenants that lead to teaching kids that we live in a systematically racist country."

Leo Terrel, himself a former history teacher and presently a civil rights attorney, went on *Fox and Friends* to further educate Ms. Weingarten. He stated, "Look, it's very clear that 1607 and 1619 and the slave issue was discussed and being discussed in American history, but to make the premise that the American Revolution was fought on slavery is an outright lie. And I submit to you that this union president was afraid of losing her job if she said the wrong thing." Then he added, "It's very insulting because what's at issue here is not only the credibility of American history but lying to our school children about American history. This is what's so frightening about this Critical Race Theory."

In conclusion, he said, "In the American Revolution, we fought against the British for our independence, not to preserve slavery. That is a lie, and yes, that union president is afraid." He is absolutely right. What is happening in the illusory land of

Wokeism is exactly what transpired inside the Soviet Union and within its satellites in education. Only very few brave people had the courage to overcome the intellectual terror of the regime and speak the truth. For questioning the official version of history, I was kicked out of three high schools in Hungary.

Vilifying and lying about the past and the present and worshiping an unreal future have been the modus operandi of the so-called progressive semi-intellectuals from times immemorial. In the same vein, Black Lives Matter, Antifa, other like-minded groups, and today's Democrat Party have been determined to erase the past, besmirch the present with lies, and promise a future in which the victims will become the rulers by meting out the Biblical "eye for an eye and tooth for a tooth" punishment.

Thus, the dictum that the hate-filled and violent striving for a utopian society is innocuous has been belied by many sordid examples in history. The most recent example of an abusively hubristic ideology is Marxism with its mendaciously phony "Dialectic Materialism" and "Scientific Socialism." Actually, Marxism is a fake pseudo-ideology. In reality, it is a "means to justify the ends" collection of cruel and destructive tactics designed to cause an abundance of horribly egregious human suffering. The ultimate objective has always been to allow a small minority to take absolute control of a society by seizing all levels of the government behind a deceptively attractive lie.

The late Russian Nobel Prize winner author Alexander Solzhenitsyn perceptively described the evils of the Soviet

Union's pathological herd mentality in his many novels. In *The First Circle* (V Kruge Pervom), one of his characters, Lev Rubin, states that Stalin's crimes were fully justified and were inevitable by the Marxist/Leninist/Stalinist promise of the glorious classless future in which absolute equality, social justice, and unimaginable prosperity would reign. In the *Gulag Archipelago* (Arkhipelag GULAG), Solzhenistsyn compares truth and what he calls "ideological lie." According to him, "ideological lie" is evil justification for violence and mayhem, and in the final instance, it is more destructive to the mentality and integrity of the soul than naked and unbridled terror.

Americans across the nation and lawmakers in every state must decisively respond to the blatant lies and outlandish idiocies of the Democrat Party and its extremist "Sturmtruppen." In order to save America, the ultimate objective of every patriotic American must be not to contain but to destroy these pathological liars. Black Lives Matter and Antifa's penchant for violence places them squarely outside the law. Otherwise, the war on domestic terrorism against these pathological psychopaths will remain pretty endless. Moreover, the overwhelming majority of Americans will feel no longer at home in their own country. Finally, if this pathological and sociopathic mentality is not eliminated, short-term political calculations resulting in permanent instability and chaos will destroy the United States of America.

The enduring but limited appeal of Black Lives Matter, Antifa, and the most extremist wing of the Democrat Party has sprang not from the veracity of their narrative or the unassailable logic of their convoluted thinking but rather from the negative emotions of those who have felt betrayed by the political establishment and have sought new champions whom they believed could feel their "pain" and understand their grievances. Another factor in their thinking has been their disdain for politicians in general. Even the Democrat Party has been considered to be as an unacceptable collection of modernizing social Democrats and traditional left-wingers imitating Marxist ideas.

Ayanna Pressley, a member of the so-called Squad, said when addressing those who refuse to integrate into American society, "Anyone who is interested in building a more equitable and just world is a part of the Squad." This rejectionist mentality has been mainly typical among immigrants who do not want to or are incapable of feeling American because of the large cultural differences or the conscious spurning of American values.

In reality, it is impossible to measure how many first- and second-generation immigrants think that the values of the United States of America are not being correctly applied to them, but assimilation versus identity politics has become a central issue in the Democrat Party's rhetoric. However, assimilation versus identity politics has not been the central problem. The most important national debate has always been about the core principles of national identity and intolerance in inter-communal relations.

Clearly, the principles of freedom and equality have been gradually eroding as the challenges of domestic terrorism, counter-terrorism, illegal immigration, and economic uncertainties have mounted. When President Trump began to tackle these challenges head-on, he encountered fierce opposition. The Biden Administration clearly tries to avoid addressing these challenges decisively. Soaring illegal immigration, high crime rates in Democrat-controlled cities and states, frequent clashes with police who are relentlessly maligned by the domestic terrorists of Black Lives Matter and Antifa, and ritual burning of buildings and cars mainly in the North-East and West Coasts states have been daily occurrences.

The Biden Administration's economic incompetence, the sick pursuit of "diversity" at any cost in the government that put unprofessional and inexperienced political nobodies in decision-making positions, and the proliferating avalanche of senseless regulations filled with ideological extremism as well as self-protective castes will only exacerbate the already tense situation.

For all of those reasons, the lasting legacy of the Declaration of Independence, the American Revolution, and the Constitution combined carry the weight of the history of the United States of America. This glorious albeit imperfect past is the present too and will have to remain the foundation of the future greatness of America.

The Trump presidency and the Democrat Party's full-scale resistance to it have changed many things, possibly for a long time in the American political culture. The four years between 2017 and 2021 were, as Charles Dickens put it, the best and the worst times. Economically, until the COVID-19 pandemic struck, the Trump presidency was an unmitigated success. Politically, the utter lawlessness and the absolutely undemocratic character of the Democrat Party's opposition were a destructive curse both domestically as well as internationally for the United States of America.

The ruthless violence and mayhem unleashed with the enthusiastic support of the Democrats and the media climaxed in fearsome terror vehemently concealed and denied by them. The reason for this politically motivated camouflage was to hide the ugly truth about the true nature of the ruthless Democrat Party machine and its deceptive claims for superiority in wisdom as well as moral fortitude. Largely undetected by the average American, the Democrat Party's behavior foreshadowed the Biden Administration's political totalitarianism to legitimize the ruthless actions against its foes, real or imagined.

In the middle of a global domestic meltdown caused by the Socialist/Communist initiatives of the Biden Administration, Americans will have to take stock of their decision in November 2022. Based on the occurrences and experiences of the first four months, the Unifier-in-Chief and his administration is completely out of step with the overwhelming majority of the nation. Having claimed a mandate not unlike many of his predecessors, President Biden is clearly not the right person to occupy the highest elected office in the United States of America. Although the elections resulted in a small majority for Democrats in the House of Representatives and a tie in the Senate, his electoral victory over President Trump remains suspect. Only the future will tell whether the elections were rigged or not. From day one of his inauguration, his administration has gotten down to work on an almost endless list of long-standing left-wing aspirations, deliberating mainly in secret so as to give nothing away, even to their closest congressional and local associates.

Like in the American horror movie series called *Puppet Master*, President Biden's puppet masters in the White House have modeled his administration after this radical and threatening storyline. Today, this brainless and extreme radicalism is in shambles. The economy is stalling, unemployment is rising, the irrational demands of the extreme radicals are becoming more destructive, the federal government is paralyzed by Wokeism, illegal immigration is illimitable, and the international environment grows rapidly more chaotic and threatening.

Battered by the sudden avalanche of mostly self-made crises, the Biden Administration resembles an exhausted warrior fighting to death for its politically narrow and destructive ends. The end result can be foreseen even at this early stage of the Biden presidency. Whether Joe Biden will be able to serve out his entire term or whether the even more incompetent and inexperienced

Kamala Harris with her hyena-like laughter will take over, the Biden presidency will surely end in catastrophic defeat and as of yet unimaginable political as well as economic disarray because of its persistent refusal to face reality. The combination of President Biden's burgeoning dementia and his puppet masters' extreme radicalism will continue to prevent them from resolving the inherent conflicts rooted in the past and the present. This dire prediction is also supported by the Biden Administration's lack of a reality-based narrative that could enable the majority of Americans to rally for an American cause and live up to their view of themselves.

This impending national catastrophe is compounded by the rising ethnic, cultural, and religious tensions in which education has become an unnecessary theater of war far removed from the original ideal of it being the unifying foundation of the United States of America. Because of the Democrat Party's unconditional embrace of the fallacious doctrines of "White supremacy," "systematic and institutionalized racism," "identity politics," "Cancel Culture," "Critical Race Theory," and the slogan "No Justice, No Peace," the educational system is no longer the crucible of American identity; it has become a battleground for artificial ideological diversity fought over by increasingly incompetent politicians and mostly irrational educators.

The economy, the center of ubiquitous concern for all Americans, especially amidst the COVID-19 pandemic, has been averse to the Biden administration's efforts to promote growth, which was dominant under the Trump administration. Having declared that a million new jobs had likely been created in April 2021 by the Biden-worshipping bunch of economists and even enthusiastic employers, American businesses only hired 266,000 new workers—clearly way below the predicted job numbers. Again contradicting the facts, President Biden grandiloquently declared, "You might think we should be disappointed," which was the natural reaction of every sane individual. Of course, in President Biden's delusional and mentally inhibited world, these numbers only show that his administration's "American Rescue Plan was designed to help us over the course of the year, not 60 days."

While the New York Stock Exchange is gyrating up and down with the speed of a missile and profit margins have been below those before the pandemic, President Biden triumphantly stated, "Today, there is more evidence our economy is moving in the right direction." To further demonstrate his incompetence and mental decline, he added, "This is progress. This is a testament to our new strategy. We've got work to do, to state the obvious, we have work to do." Exceptionally, this latter part of his statement is true.

Unemployment benefits in the Democrat-controlled states surpass wages, inflation is on the rise, and the index for houses, used cars, and trucks rose 10 percent in April. The food index increased in April as well, rising 0.4 percent. The index for all items minus food and energy rose 0.9 percent in April, its largest monthly increase since April 1982. The all-items index rose 4.2 percent for the 12 months ending in April, an increase larger than the 2.6 percent increase for the period ending in March.

The energy index will also increase because of the ransom cyberattack on the Colonial Pipeline. The pipeline, which transports nearly half of the East Coast's fuel supplies up from Texas, had been turned off because of a ransom cyberattack by a group of presumably professional Russian-government-controlled hackers. Almost simultaneously, the Islamic Republic of Iran has embarked on its irregular warfare shenanigans by unleashing Hamas, one of its many proxies in the Sunni world, on Israel to force the weak Biden Administration's hand in Vienna, Austria.

In the south, illegal immigration went up drastically in April, surpassing 178,000 illegal immigrants entering the U.S. By the way, this represents a nearly tenfold increase from 2020 and way above the 2019 surge at the Mexican border. While the governor of Arizona demands the removal of the vice president from her elevated position as the Immigration Tsar and the polls indicate only 43 percent support for President Biden's open border idiocy, his administration has done nothing to curb the assault of the Central and South American gangs against the sovereignty of the United States of America, which he swore to uphold.

Instead of admitting his error to oppose President Trump's strict immigration policies, President Biden doubled down on his open border policy by incessantly lying about the facts. While reports about the chaos on the southern border have multiplied, he has steadfastly maintained, "The truth of the matter is, nothing has changed. It happens every single, solitary year. There is a significant increase in the number of people coming to the border in the winter months of January, February, March. That happens every year."

Of course, his statement is a bald-faced lie. When caught, President Biden opined thus, "Look. I inherited a god-awful mess from Trump at the border." The question is whether it is also President Trump's fault that illegal immigrants come to the United States of America wearing T-shirts with the words "Biden Let Us In, You Promised." And is it President Trump's fault that human smugglers and coyotes tell the gullible and desperate illegal immigrants that Biden is their friend and has opened the borders to everyone who wants to enter the territory of the United States of America with absolute impunity? Finally, is it President Trump's fault that illegal immigration is spurred by all of the social and medical benefits promised by Democrats to everyone who succeeds in reaching America? Of course not. President Biden attempts to preach to people who hover between the real world and an illusionary one. These useful idiots comprise his political base and are his ethical camouflage to lie.

To illustrate the incompetence, unprofessionalism, and hypocrisy of President Biden and his administration, Fox News reported on May13, 2021, that "the Biden administration will resume border wall construction" as the allegedly nonexistent border crisis worsens. According to Fox News, the United States

Army Corps of Engineers (USACE) will restart construction on a 13.4 mile stretch of levee in the Rio Grande Valley. The decision reportedly follows pressure from local residents and politicians to mend the incessant crossing surge.

To further demonstrate the complete idiocy of the Biden administration, the Department of Homeland Security (DHS) stated that repairs will "protect border communities from physical dangers" left in the wake of the construction. The statement also claims that "large holes" were blown into the Rio Grande Valley's flood barrier system to make way for the wall which, as a result, requires repairing to prevent "catastrophic flooding." Again, lies upon lies.

The mayor of Del Rio, Texas, Democrat Bruno Lozano sounded off on *Fox & Friends* on May 12, 2021, expressing his concern for the worsening crisis and the Biden administration's failure to control it. He said, "They keep telling us that the border is under control, and I simply do not understand how with a 392% increase this fiscal year alone." Then he continued, "Last year, we had 19,724 captures at this point, and right now, we're at 97,398. I simply do not understand how that's under control."

Another Biden idiocy is HR-1, the brainchild of the House of Representatives to unconstitutionally federalize the election laws. While simultaneously relentlessly attacking other states for their new voting laws, the Biden administration maintains that HR-1 is constitutional when it is not and labels Florida and Georgia as racist Republican states. Andrea Young, executive director of the

ACLU in Georgia, claimed, "This terrible bill was drafted as a direct swipe at Georgians' participating in the Black Lives Matter protest who are asserting their constitutional rights."

What the Biden administration, the Democrat Party, Black Lives Matter, Antifa, and similar groups intend to accomplish in the United States of America is emotional hostage-taking of the overwhelming majority of Americans for the sake of turning the entire nation into prisoners of the past. The belief of the Constitution as a model for the United States of America and the world has also been attacked by the race-baiting minority as indefensible because of its morally reprehensible racist overtone. If past and present realities contradict such a false and distorted vision, if its adherents favor rejecting sanity for a completely false narrative about the United States of America, if they prefer to reject freedom for their fantastically unreal oppressive ideals, and if they vociferously oppose national unity for tribal fragmentation, it will leave them feeling deprived of their inherent rights and render them willing to embrace radical extremism as well as violent illusions. In this La La Land of unrealities, compromise is worse than murder, and factional, tribal, personal, and ideological conflicts are demanded as a must to bring about a fundamental transformation of the nation. Recourse to bloody violence is mandatory.

To decisively stop and reverse this destructive idiocy, in 2017, an exceptional outsider attempted to unify the opposing forces around a strong state. In 2021, he was defeated by Democrats who have thrived on disunity and social instability for the last six decades. Yet, the unfinished business of straightening out the ship of the nation sailing forward in stormy seas must be completed by the enlightened reason of the founding principles of the United States of America.

To set against such destructive idiocy is the swelling backlash by the sane majority. One by one, the idiocies of the Democrat Party and its Sturmtruppen that have underpinned their lying narratives are falling by the wayside in an accelerated fashion. Multitudes of labor organizations have been losing membership with staggering speed. Presently, only 9 percent of the American workforce belongs to various trade unions. Teaching trade unions, which have resisted reform, quickly politicized the COVID-19 pandemic, and enjoyed the powerful political backing of the Democrat Party to which they have contributed their votes and money, are being resisted and even ridiculed by a growing number of parents as well as students.

The mounting tensions between parents and teachers has escalated across the nation. Homeschooling and enrollment at private schools have steadily risen to account for 25 percent or almost 6 million PK-12 students. Loudoun County, Virginia, the richest county in the nation, has fallen to the idiotic lies of the most radical and extremist wing of the Democrat Party.

On *Fox & Friends First*, Elizabeth Perrin and Joe Mobley, both residents of the county, blasted a graphic book that was being peddled to children at their school. Calling it "despicable,"

Mr. Mobley said that outraged parents are united in their rejection of books about Critical Race Theory, demanding "an all-out ban on the curriculum." He went on to complain, "They have books that are supposed to be teaching–, you know. It is a language that we can't say here but very sexually explicit stuff, stuff that if any children in the classrooms (which is very likely) have experienced sexual trauma, it would put them back into that place and really stuff the kids shouldn't be readings that came in under the auspices of COVID and not following the procurement procedures."

Outside of Loudoun County, parents throughout the state of Virginia torched their schoolboards over Critical Race Theory and sexually explicit teachings. Even among Black parents, the consensus is that Critical Race Theory is not honest and objective history but a tactic also used by the Ku Klux Klan on slavery many years ago to dumb down Blacks in order to prevent them from thinking for themselves.

Today, a national movement is growing in opposition to teaching children to hate America. According to NBC News, a group of House Republicans has taken action by introducing a pair of bills to ban diversity training for federal employees and the military. The NBC News report claimed that "some 30 GOP representatives have signed on to support both the Combating Racist Training in the Military Act and the Stop Critical Race Theory Act." The realization that Critical Race Theory is a divisive ideology that threatens to poison the American psyche is finally gaining force. As Congressman Dan Bishop of North Caroline stated, "For the sake of our children's future, we must stop this effort to cancel the truth of our founding and our country."

These federal bills are only the latest examples of already adapted or proposed legislations to oppose the pseudo-diversity and false anti-racism teaching in the majority of states across the United States of America. Idaho, Oklahoma, Louisiana, Rhode Island, and Tennessee have already targeted the teaching of the poisonous Critical Race Theory.

Most recently, the Virginia GOP lieutenant governor nominee slammed Critical Race Theory curriculum as "nonsense." Ms. Winsome Sears, the first Black female Republican to participate in the race, told *Fox & Friends* that "It's going to be detrimental to our schools and not what we want. It supposedly is to help someone who looks like me, and I'm sick of it. I'm sick of being used by the Democrats, and so are many people who look like me."

Former Education Secretary Betsy DeVos also denounced the American Federation of Teachers President Randi Weingarten for the latter's aggressive promotion of the 1619 Project. On Martha McCallum's show *The Story,* she opined, "Let's be really clear. The 1619 Project is not history. [...] It denies 1776 and our constitution and our founding documents and the goal of forming a more perfect union."

Even *The New York Times* has felt pressure from the outraged public. Charlie Warzel, a *Times* columnist who claims to be an expert in "online radicalization," warned his readers not to "go down the rabbit hole" in a February 18, 2021, op-ed. Further down in his writing, he also admonished his readers not to succumb to "wrongthink" regarding race and history. It appears that Jen Psaki, President Biden's spokesperson, has not gotten the message. At her May 12, 2021, press conference, she was asked about a proposal by Arkansas Senator Tom Cotton's opposition to schools teaching subjects like the 1619 Project and Critical Race Theory. Her answer showed that the Democrat Party intends to latch onto the dry bone of racism in America slogan indefinitely, "I don't think we would think that educating the youth and next and future leaders of the country of systematic racism is indoctrination. That is actually responsible."

Again, Laura Ingraham is right. On *The Ingraham Angle,* she first ripped into President Biden and the Democrats "for their obsession to push a radical ideology" with "shiny objects" while being "disinterested in solving the problems facing Middle America." Then she said, "The fact is, it's painfully obvious that Democrats and their media flunkies are totally disinterested in solving the problems facing middle America. If you drive less because gas is too high, good. They hate your big SUVs anyway. If you have fewer kids because the cost of living is so high, good. They hate big families. If the cost of guns is prohibitive and there's a shortage of ammo, good. They want to gut the Second Amendment. If you're worried about more crime and less police, too bad. And it's all the cops fault anyway—they're racist."

The fact is that the United States of America is in a crisis because the Democrat Party, and to a lesser extent the Republican Party as well, are in political, ideological, and intellectual disarray. The real reasons for these crises mainly lie in the domestic arena. For the Democrat Party, the initial acceptance of its anti-Trumpism is fading rapidly. To add insult to injury, the majority of the American people have grown frustrated and angry about the violence, destruction, and the Biden administration's glaring idiotic ideology triggered incompetence. For many, this incompetence is coupled with the rapidly growing powers of a miniscule but aggressively extremist wing of the Democrat Party. The latter threatens a split within the party.

The average Democrat voter is angry about the inner destruction of their party and the results it brought to the nation. They also resent the Democrat Party's alliance with neo-racist movements and organizations. The combination of these factors has alienated many former members of the Democrat establishment. As a result, there is growing disappointment of their abandonment by the Democrat Party. All of these negative trends are compounded by the fact that the leader of the Democrat Party is mentally demented. His unpresidential demeanor and sharp veering away from his electoral program of unity and healing immediately after having been inaugurated have left him without a political or human spine. Because of that, they do not see a promising future for their party.

In the Republican Party, the internal opposition by a small minority who believes in having been anointed to protect the nonexistence legacy of the two Bushes is annoying to the vast majority of Republican members as well as independent voters. These intra-party disagreements are rooted in the Republican cause itself. George W. Bush's sentimental "compassionate conservatism" oscillated for eight years between President Reagan's hard realism and the conservative intellectuals desire to be accepted by the liberal establishment in academia. President Trump's businesslike toughness and his combative rhetoric certainly ran against their twin desires. More and more Americans believe establishment politicians are corrupt and desire a strong chief executive. For an increasing number of Americans, the fact that the United States of America is not what it used to be—or what they want it to be—is the most important factor in their political decisions.

Where do all of these dysfunctions leave the United States of America and its citizenry? It leaves them in a vacuum. For as Prince Metternich said, "A lie is a vacuum," and many lies always cause many vacuums. Amidst these crises, Americans must look in the mirror and reject all anti-American idiots who will definitely remain impervious to embracing reality versus ideologies that are based on violent mayhem and total destruction and tainted with a heap of lies. The legendary Phoenix of ancient Persia has not emerged from time to time out of the ruins of history, but it has soared high repeatedly from the life-sustaining fire of eternal and constructive renewals.

6

"WE THE PEOPLE"

BROADLY SPEAKING, THERE are two opinions about the United States of America across the globe. The minority opinion, represented by the American and international media as well as some individuals in politics and academia, holds that the United States of America has been, at least since the early 1950s, an arrogant superpower that has terrorized every state and everybody who even marginally disagreed with its dictatorial and expansionist designs. More recently, driven by the absolutely fallacious narrative of an unrepresentative, self-aggrandizing, and marauding minority as well as their puppet masters in the Democrat Party, some have claimed that the United States of America has been a racist country from its inception and is laden with hypocritical and immoral values.

Today's idiotic media Vogue du Jour, promoted aggressively without any evidence by Black Lives Matter and the Squad, is that Israel, which is unconditionally supported by the racist United States of America, has been pushing racism and dehumanization under an apartheid system against the Arab minority exactly the same way the United States of America does against Blacks and other colored minorities at home. For good measure,

Congresswoman Rashida Tlaib, whom President Biden called Rasheed, and Black Lives Matter have declared their unconditional solidarity with the Palestinians, stating, "We are a movement committed to ending settler colonialism in all forms and will continue to advocate for Palestinian liberation. Always have, and always will be. #freepalestine." The same Rashida Tlaib hijacked President Biden on May 18, 2021, at the Metropolitan Wayne County Airport in Detroit, demanding he approve the call for an immediate ceasefire by the UN Security Council and stop "Apartheid-in-Chief" Netanyahu from committing "war crimes and openly violate[ing] international law."

As could have been expected, CNN, NBC, MSNBC, and a bunch of liberal newspapers have already joined the anti-Israel orgy. Demonstrating the abysmal scholarly quality of today's higher education, Rashid Khalidi, a professor of Modern Arab Studies at Columbia University, was interviewed by the equally low IQ host of MSNBC, Joy Reid. Having likened Israel's response to Hamas' barrage of rocket attacks to the killing of African Americans during the Jim Crow era, the honorable professor mused about a movement which is supported by "social media" and Black Lives Matter, pointing out the evils committed by Israel against the supposedly innocent and defenseless Palestinian people. Not to be outdone, another so-called expert on the Middle East and Israel at MSNBC, Ali Velshi, claimed that Israel's bombing of Gaza ignores the Palestinians' right to exist. This so-called journalist forgot to mention the initial Palestinian provocations and the more general truth that the Palestinians openly brag about their intention of killing all of the Jews in Israel and beyond.

Ironically, when they are providing their opinion about an enduring and complex problem thousands of miles away from the East Coast, the arrogance of these Monday-morning quarterbacks is really humbling. What these shallow-minded journalists will never comprehend is that by reducing hardly solvable problems to extremely simplistic talking points, they exacerbate the problem rather than contribute to the solution of the situation. What usually follows is a comparison between the oppressed and victimized American minorities and the equally oppressed and victimized Arabs, erroneously called Palestinians, in Israel. From here on, they all climb the Olympian height of progressive morality and condemn the United States of America and Israel as immoral for being stronger and smarter than those who have sworn to annihilate all of its White as well as Jewish inhabitants. So unfair, so immoral, so unjust, and so idiotic.

On the Virginia side of the Potomac, Lt. Col. Matthew Lohmeier stated that the Pentagon, headed by Lloyd Austin who is Black, sent servicemembers a video claiming that America and White people are "evil." In early February 2021 just days after his confirmation by the Senate, the same secretary of defense ordered a nationwide military standdown aimed at fighting "domestic extremism in the ranks." On his podcast, Lt. Col. Lohmeier also stated, "The diversity, inclusion, and equity industry and the training(s) we are receiving in the military [...] is rooted in Critical Race Theory, which is rooted in Marxism." Finally, in his self-published book, he said that a "neo-Marxist agenda" has taken hold on the top brass in the Pentagon and warned in a comment directed at Austin that "this agenda, it will divide us; it will not unify us."

Against the primitive, uninformed, and malicious media and politically motivated lies, there is the truth about the American nation with its exceptionally inspiring history, its multitude of civilized values, its multiethnicity, its diverse and deep Judeo-Christian morality, and essential decency. Personally, I have been in almost every state and territory of the world in either an official or business capacity. My experiences have led me to a single conclusion—there is no better place to call home than the United States of America.

When I escaped Hungary in January 1973, the Federal Republic of Germany granted me political asylum, but in the natives' minds, I remained a foreigner, an *Auslaender* in German. Based on a single lecture at the George Washington University in Washington, D.C., I was invited to an advisory and research position at the Library of Congress and was subsequently loaned out to the Supreme Court of the United States of America as well as the Reagan White House.

My articles and essays appeared in quick succession in newspapers, Library of Congress publications, and Congressional Records. Throughout my government employment and while in private business, I have never encountered any discrimination. I was never called a "foreigner" or any other discriminatory name. From day one, I have been accepted as an equal, regardless of the fact that I was not born in America. My two beautiful children, Peter and Judith, were flawlessly integrated into society, and today, they are happily married. Their children are proud Americans with bright futures.

As a few examples of my experiences, I would like to briefly indulge my readers' attention. My son Peter was in 8th grade in Cooper Intermediary School in McLean, Virginia, when his social studies teacher quite emotionally (and one-sidedly, I might add) criticized the federal and the state governments for their insufficient financial assistance for the poor. My son was three years old when we left Hungary and spent over four years in Germany where the Hausmeister repeatedly called him *Auslaender*. He stood up and explained to his uninformed teacher that his father was a penniless refugee who never asked for or accepted handouts from any government.

In another instance, we moved into our new house in Langley McLean in broad daylight. We did not know our new neighbors. While my friends and I were emptying the U-Haul truck, my wife shepherded our two small children into the still-empty house. When we were almost finished with unpacking everything, one of our neighbors showed up with a complete meal for as many as eight people. Remarking that she noticed the two small children, she opined that we must be very tired and offered to take them to her house overnight. Her offer sounded more like a command that we naturally could not refuse. We lived in the same house for almost 40 years. After getting to know all of the neighbors, we were fortified in our belief of America and its people's inherent goodness.

When one of President Reagan's special assistants requested that the Library of Congress loan me to the White House, I got to know the president as well as the vice president. During my three years there, I also met most of the cabinet members. I never encountered anything but kindness and respect for my person and opinions. The same applied to members of Congress in both Houses and their staffs. Whenever I traveled to any state or congressional district to speak, I only met kindness and respect. In addition, I was able to witness firsthand that America is the most moral nation on earth. As opposed to Hungary where corruption is a national sport, I never experienced anything close to official or private corruption. When on vacation and meeting people across the nation, I realized how civilized the American people are with their deep-seated Judeo-Christian values.

Having traveled extensively as an American official, one experience stands out. It happened in August 1989, just a month after the bloody suppression of the Tiananmen Square uprising in Beijing, which spread across the People's Republic of China. The then Chinese Ambassador Han Xu in Washington, D.C., who was an admirer of Hungarian literature and music, called me up. He complained about the sanctions imposed by Congress and proposed that a delegation of congressional staffers should visit his country and meet with its leaders. Following the approval by congressional leaders, six of us flew to Beijing accompanied by the charge d'affaires Dr. Shaw via his home town of Shanghai.

We arrived around 5:30 a.m. on a Sunday and were immediately driven to the Beijing Hotel, two blocks away from the ominous Tiananmen Square. Following a short nap, we were taken to the Forbidden City to meet with then Chinese Foreign Minister Qian Qichen. Joined by our Ambassador James Lilly, we were ushered into a large rectangular room. At the far end of the room, Mr. Qian was flanked by two young interpreters. Criticizing Congress for imposing sanctions with a flowery Chinese sentence, "Those who tied the knots must also untie them," he uttered the following, "The People's Republic of China is a democracy. The United States of America is a dictatorship." In the same vein, he went on rambling about Chinese kindness while simultaneously trashing America for being the vilest colonial power in human history.

About 45 minutes later, I raised my hand. Mr. Qian stopped, and I said the following, "Mr. Foreign Minister, we listened to your speech for 45 minutes. Allow me to take the same amount of time to reply. As far as your assertion is concerned that China is a democracy and America is a dictatorship, let me quote the first three words from the Preamble of our Constitution—'We The People.' As Frederick Douglass, an ex-slave and abolitionist remarked in 1860, 'it's [referring to the constitution] language is we the people; not we the white people. Not even we the citizens, not we the privileged class, not we the high, not we the low, but we the people.' In your constitution, the real sovereign is the Communist Party and not the Chinese people. Thus, the People's Republic of China is not a democracy. It is a dictatorship of the Chinese Communist Party par excellence. To me as a former refugee from a Communist country where the dictatorship of the Communist Party has been much milder than in your country, these differences between the depositories of sovereignty are crucial. Therefore, in opposition to your statement, I tell you that the United States of America is the best democracy that the world has ever had." Unexplainably, at the end of my rebuttal, I received a standing ovation from our Chinese hosts. From that first meeting on, no Chinese official at our subsequent meetings for almost a month ever compared the People's Republic of China and the United States of America in Mr. Qian's misleading way from Xian, Shanghai, Guangzhou, to Haikou onto Hainan Island.

The moral of this story is that the real challenge is to always employ the truth against lying people. Most importantly, it is not enough not to lose the battles but to win the war. Secondarily, preemption is the best intellectual weapon against loathsome people. Finally, these loathsome individuals, who are always filled with ample hatred, are always intellectually corrupt and unscrupulously immoral as well. Therefore, exposing their insidious doubletalk will reveal the indefensibility of their lies.

Too many Americans in politics, academia, and the media are prone to forget that these three words at the beginning of the Preamble do not contain only rights but also come with mandatory obligations. The most important responsibility of every citizen is his or her personal duty to make informed decisions. In order to be informed, every citizen must be educated. The Founding Fathers firmly believed that in order to participate responsibly and fully in the affairs of the republic, citizens must educate themselves on important policy issues to qualify as informed voters. Education, in turn, means a combination of institutionalized as well as individual education. Moreover, education presupposes objective instructions by teachers free of political as well as intellectual bias.

Regrettably, the Biden administration's education priority is federalized indoctrination by shamelessly catering to anti-American thoughts as well as unscientific neo-racist nonsense. Encouraging public schools to teach the 1619 Project and offer grants to various other historical lies, such as Critical Race Theory by Ibram X. Kendy and other neo-racist apostles of anti-Americanism, will only mean a massive and Democrat Party-controlled political disinformation campaign focused on intellectually vulnerable children. In addition, it will also mean the dumbing down of future generations.

The Biden education credo has been well summarized by the above mentioned Ibram X. Kendi, "The defining question is whether the discrimination is creating equity or inequality. If discrimination is creating equity, it is anti-racist. If discrimination is creating inequality, then it is racist. [...] The only remedy to racist discrimination is antiracist discrimination. The only remedy to past discrimination is present discrimination. The only remedy to present discrimination is future discrimination."

What an idiotic collection of intellectual rubbish! What a depraved mind! What a destructive way of thinking! To start with, according to the Cambridge Dictionary, equity is "the situation in which everyone is treated fairly and equally: a society based on equity and social justice." Before answering the question whether "everyone is treated fairly and equally" in America, Ibram X. Kendy immediately switches to discrimination. Thus in his distorted universe, fairness and equality are nonexistent in America. What really exists, according to him, is discrimination. When discrimination creates equity, it is antiracist which means that fairness and equality do not apply when they are employed to discriminate against individuals who are deemed to be judged by him as racist and thus undeserving of protection. Moreover, since there has never been absolute fairness and equality in history, discrimination on behalf of every person who considers himself or herself a victim or is judged by him to be a victim enjoys the benefits of reverse discrimination in perpetuity, "The only remedy for past discrimination is present discrimination. The only remedy for present discrimination is future discrimination."

Clearly, this is not the United States of America in which the overwhelming majority of Americans, including future generations, want to live. And clearly, it does not resemble the United States of America that the Founding Fathers and successive generations have been fighting for. According to James McHenry, as Benjamin Franklin famously remarked when Elizabeth Willing Powel asked about the form of government that he and his colleagues agreed upon, "Republic, if you can keep it" was the answer. Whether Dr. Franklin uttered those words or not, the dilemma facing the United States of America today is aptly summarized in this short sentence. Can common sense and sanity prevail amidst the relentless onslaught of the race-baiting miniscule minority, or would America as we have known it be destroyed by these idiots?

Historically, the trial of Socrates in 399 BC closely resembles the present situation in American society. Socrates was charged with two capital offenses: asebeia and impiety against the pantheon of Athens and corrupting the minds of the youth. As background information to the trial, one must mention that at the beginning of the fourth century BC, Sparta gained the upper hand over Athens in the long-lasting Peloponnesian War. In 404 B.C., Athens surrendered to Sparta and became part of Sparta's Empire. For a very short period of time, Athens was ruled by the "Thirty Tyrants." In 403 B.C., democracy was restored by Thrasybulus.

Socrates, who claimed to be a patriot, was, according to Plato, a "gadfly" of Athens. Compared with today's neo-racist socio-paths, Socrates was an advocate of social justice too. However, based on Xenophon of Athens' account, Socrates believed that he was "the gods' gift" to the Athenian people. In other words, he was convinced that he alone was on "the right side of history." Thus, in spite of the biased accounts of Plato and Xenophon as well as many more recent interpreters of Socrates' dialogues and trial, he espoused "social justice" theories to the detriment of the democratic principles that governed Athens for almost a century.

Most prominently, he claimed that a privileged and educated few, called a vanguard by Marx and Lenin, is more capable of governing than the citizens of the city state. In a similar vein, America's neo-racists have behaved in the same narcissistic way and have advocated views that are fundamentally contrary to the democratic principles upon which the United States of America was founded and has been governed for almost 250 years. They have clearly presented themselves as self-anointed heirs and prophets of social justice in the mode of Socrates, Marx, Lenin, Gandhi, Martin Luther King, Mandela, Nkhruma, and Kenyatta. Their logic has not acknowledged any political or intellectual boundaries. In their egomaniac frenzy, they have propagated wholesale destruction without offering new solutions. For them, personal aggrandizement has been more important than their misguided ideas of world redemption. They have systematically disregarded the human toll that their divisive and even hateful rhetoric has extracted from those whom they hypocritically wanted to rescue from inequality and social injustice.

A recent prime example of such narcissistic and destructive behavior has been Dr. Anthony Fauci's Napoleonic peacock dance across the American as well as the international media. First disseminating contradictory opinions about how to fight the pandemic, then lying about his and his organization's involvement in the by now infamous Wuhan laboratory's joint "gain-of-function" research, and finally coming to the idiotic conclusion that the COVID-19 pandemic has exposed the "undeniable effects of racism" on the Black community, Dr. Fauci proved his incapability to remain in the forefront of the fight against the deadly virus. Slyly, Dr. Fauci has been silent about the origins of the coronavirus and his as well as his colleagues possible complicity in this worldwide existential catastrophe while blaming "White supremacy" and "systematic and institutionalized racism" as the main reasons of the alleged victimization of Blacks during the pandemic.

As Socrates was rightly charged for corrupting the Athenian youth, Dr. Fauci must be exposed as a total professional fraud and an intellectual misfit. Idiots have always had all the wrong answers to real problems. Idiots have always created a pseudo-reality for the people in order to hide their incompetence. Idiots have always disregarded facts and created a make-believe universe of lies and deceptions.

Speaking of corrupting the youth, one must return to the war over the hearts and minds of young Americans, starting with their evil indoctrination by sociopathic educators from kindergarten to graduate school. The first salvo has been fired by the so-called "progressives." The 1619 Project by Nikole Hanna-Jones tries to reinvent the past as an uninterrupted cavalcade of "White supremacy," entirely characterized by the oppression of the noble Black minority by the inherently evil White majority. Claiming that the founding of America was in 1619 when the first slaves arrived on the shores of the colonies, the 1619 Project makes an intellectual fool and a factual liar of the author and all those who support it. Denying that the true founding of the United States of America was on July 4, 1776, is nothing but ahistorical filth.

As Conor Friederdorf's January 6, 2020, article in *The Atlantic* states, "1776 honors America's diversity in a way 1619 does not." He continued, charging the 1619 Project of "reframe(ing) history, rejecting the centrality of 1776 and instead understanding 1619 as our true founding and placing the consequences of slavery and the contributions of Black Americans at very center of the story we tell ourselves about who we are." Irredeemably false. Those poor black Africans who were sold by their own tribal chiefs to Arab and European slave traders for goods produced outside of Africa were absolutely illiterate, and except their tribal and clannish customs, they lacked culture and civilization. Their utility was purely economical.

As other persons forced into slavery from times immemorial, these wretched souls historically constituted the
cheapest labor in every society. As abominable as the institution of slavery has been, persons forced into slavery were overwhelmingly uneducated people. As far as the United States of
America was concerned, they played a very marginal political
role across the 13 colonies. Neither were they in any shape or
form involved in the work of the First and Second Continental
Congresses in 1774 and 1776 respectively (the latter now known
as the Constitutional Convention), including the writing of the
Declaration of Independence and subsequent drafting of the
Constitution in 1787. Moreover, the 1619 Project is also replete
with many other major inaccuracies, especially concerning the
Indigenous People. For all of these reasons, the 1619 Project is
absolutely unfit as teaching material for early American history.

This disgraceful and self-serving distortion of American
history prompted President Trump to initiate "The President's
Advisory 1776 Commission." Led by Hillsdale College President
Larry Arnn, the Commission's final report emphasized "patriotic
education," and its aims to cultivate "a better education among
Americans in the principles and history of our nation." In its
introduction, the report states the objective of the Commission
was to "enable a rising generation to understand the history and
principles of the founding of the United States in 1776 and to
strive to form a more perfect Union." To make this objective a
reality, the introduction calls for the "restoration of American

education, which can only be grounded on a history of those principles that are accurate, honest, unifying, inspiring, and ennobling."

Indeed, as Alexis de Tocqueville said in *Democracy in America*, "In the United States, the sum of men's education is directed toward politics." The emphasis was on education and not indoctrination. The difference between the two processes is that real education presupposes absolute freedom of information, while indoctrination is a violation of the former. Bluntly stated, indoctrination is intellectual totalitarianism designed to deny by psychological or physical force unencumbered access to knowledge deemed inimical to a single arbitrary doctrine. The real threat to human senity is that, if allowed, intellectual totalitarianism has always degenerated into political totalitarianism that has consumed every individual's mind and body throughout history. Thus, if today's neo-racist idiocy is not decisively eliminated, the present and future generations will grow up together with the gradual death of humanity.

In the United States of America, the uninterrupted path to the educational revolution commenced between 1782 and 1802 with the establishment of 19 colleges that exist to this day. According to Frederick Rudoph, the accepted view was "the colleges were now serving a new responsibility to a new nation: the preparation of young men for responsible citizenship in a republic that must prove itself, the preparation for lives of usefulness of young men who also intended to prove themselves."

The matter of republican education was a main topic among the Founding Fathers. George Washington, James Madison, Noah Webster, and other notable founders were interested in the quality of higher education. Thomas Jefferson, John Witherspoon, Benjamin Rush, and Benjamin Franklin were all actively involved in the establishment, leadership, and funding of colleges and academies. For President Jefferson, education was a duty of every citizen for constantly developing American democracy. Therefore, for him and his fellow compatriots, education and liberty were inseparable. To quote him directly on how to avoid tyranny, he suggested thus, "to illuminate, as far as practicable, the minds of the people at large."

In his 1797 *Remarks on Education* for the American Philosophical Society, Samuel Harrison Smith mentioned three reasons for republican education. Most importantly, "The citizen, enlightened, will be a free man in its truest sense." Accordingly, the citizen must know his rights and his responsibilities equally. Moreover, a thus-educated citizen will contribute to the progress and the welfare of the nation. Finally, the United States of America will be a shining example to the rest of the world by exhibiting knowledge, human dignity, and glorious intelligence. Practical deeds to develop good education were abundant across the 13 states. The Constitution of North Carolina mandated that "all useful learning shall be duly encouraged and promoted in one or more universities." Georgia, Tennessee, and Vermont all established state universities by 1800. Presidents George

Washington and Thomas Jefferson were the most avid promoters of education in general and higher education in particular.

Compared with the sorry state of many K-12 public schools and colleges, what is happening with education across the nation is disheartening and outrightly destructive. Teaching history, philosophy, religion, morality, mathematics, physics, chemistry, and even medicine has been hopelessly politicized. Identity politics, cancel culture, and Critical Race Theory have been extremely harmful to real education and the integrity of democracy in the United States of America. Fully justified pride in the countless achievements of American civilization has given way to the malicious reinterpretation and subsequent weaponization of the past.

No one deserves to be lied to. No American should be insulted by scantily educated psychopaths such as members of the Squad, other like-minded members of both Houses of Congress, and race-baiting neo-racists of Black Lives Matter, Antifa, and fellow traveler groups. They all reject national unity and prize fragmentation as well as wholesale destruction. For them, compromise is unacceptable, hatred is their philosophy, and periodic mayhem and deadly violence are means to a bloody coup d'état against the United States of America.

In these critical times in American history, it would be advisable for every American to reread President Lincoln's Gettysburg speech. His first sentence reads, "Four score and seven years ago our fathers brought forth on this continent, a new nation, conceived in liberty, and dedicated to the proposition that all men are created equal." This is the real meaning of "We the People" and the meaning American history has been the relentlessly striving toward in perfecting the United States of America. From the 10 amendments through the freeing of the slaves, the winning of two World Wars, defeating the twin evils of National Socialism and Communism, and becoming the "Shining City on the Hill" for the rest of the world, the American people have disproportionately contributed to the prosperity, peace, and the bright future as well of all mankind.

Today, however, the United States of America is in an ever-deepening constitutional, political, civilizational, and cultural crisis. American democracy is under attack and is therefore not working well. Domestically, physical violence has increased by more than 10 percent annually, at least since 2014. Racially motivated and terroristic attacks have also been on the rise. Concerns about the movement of defunding police, "death to cops" cries, and general law-and-order chaos have been overwhelming, and trust in the judiciary has been rapidly declining.

Illegal immigration, encouraged by the Democrats for purely political reasons, has contributed to a tremendous multiplication of organized gang violence and ethnic tensions. Ethnic tensions, in turn, have spilled over into violent attacks on individuals, churches, synagogues, and cultural establishments. The flames of anti-Semitism have been diligently stoked by radical extremists both within and outside of the Democrat Party. In particular, members of the Squad, mainly young and mostly illegal

Muslim immigrants, and easily gullible human trash with herd mentality have been busy to make anti-Semitism, under the guise of anti-Zionism and Israel bashing as a colonial and genocidal state, politically and culturally acceptable.

Merely 10 months after President Biden's inauguration, it has become crystal clear that the new Democrat majority does not want and is sometimes incapable of keeping most of its campaign promises. More importantly, the present occupant of the White House and his comrades in both Houses of Congress are lacking the intellect and the experience to move the United States of America in a positive direction. President Biden, Vice President Kamala Harris, and their advisors cannot see farther than the tip of their noses. They can only perceive the trees next to the White House and ignore the forest as the complex reality of a collection of trees. The beguiling promises of "unity" and domestic "peace" have never had any real content and perspective.

Consequently, the Biden administration, the speaker of the House of Representatives, and the majority leader of the Senate are engaged in a civil war against the overwhelming majority of the nation. This civil war is not fought against individuals. It is carried out against "White supremacy" in general, thus the essence of today's Democrat policies is universally personal. The question at hand for them is not whether a person is good, decent, or capable. Their classification is based on the Marxist division of people by their origin, race, upbringing, social status, type of education, and professional position. Their objective is to turn so-called victims, namely minorities, into executioners—individuals who already made their peace with violence, mayhem, and other forms of inhumanities. In this devilishly fantastic world, death is natural, but life is hopeless. Accordingly, hope becomes a shackle for the subjects of man-made totalitarianism. This is the essence of the Democrat Party's race-based policies and rhetoric.

The Democrats' ubiquitous deception campaign has been psychopathically supported by the vast majority of written and electronic media as well as Google, Facebook, Twitter, etc. Their attempts at total spiritual Gleichschaltung during the 2020 campaign have been a success. Their steady repetition of the Democrat campaign's lies and the ruthless blocking of everything that even marginally described reality resulted in a massive information vacuum. When writing or talking about President Trump and the Republicans, their reporting unfailingly dipped in shocking and frequently coarse language. On the other hand, Joe Biden was portrayed as a moderate, and Black Lives Matter as well as Antifa's violence were declared to be "largely peaceful." Thus suppressing the truth about Biden's real intentions and the reigning anarchy in the Democrat-controlled states and cities, the media has done its level best to prevent Americans from learning about the real state of affairs in their own country.

This deception, which is akin to the Soviet Union's infamous Dezinformacija campaign during the Communist dictatorship, has continued unabated, even after President Biden's January

20, 2021, inauguration. Facebook's Oversight Board upheld President Trump's ban from Facebook and Instagram, while Twitter banned the former president for months. The latter also suspended the account of California's Republican Party chairwoman for 12 days without explanation for "suspicious activity" and permanently banned conservative activist James O'Keefe.

On the other hand, Ayatollah Khamenei, a long list of anti-Semitic imams, leaders of terrorist organization worldwide, Louis Farrakhan, Turkey's president, the Chinese government, and like-minded persons, groups, and organizations appear to have Twitter's seal of approval. Similar random acts of censorship abound in other social media outlets. Most glaringly, Christian and Jewish charities have also become frequent targets of social media exile. Satirical websites that joke about Democrat politicians or so-called progressive causes have also been eliminated, many times for good from social media sites. Christian teachings about abortion, sex, and gender identities have been also punished for allegedly "inciting violence."

The examples are endless. Encouragingly, Senator Hawley introduced legislation aimed at breaking up the tech oligarchs in Silicon Valley. In Florida and many other states, legislatures and governors are spearheading legislation that will eliminate social media's totalitarian hold on the flow of information. Their efforts are commendable. Unelected CEOs and their boards should not have the absolute right to censor the opinions of the United States of America's diverse population. In this respect, the main dynamic in legislation must be the assertion of the people's sovereignty over the monopolistic position of social media outlets. Taken over by extreme radicals who have always been in a minority, Google, Facebook, Twitter, and Instagram must be open to all views, as guaranteed in the First Amendment of the Constitution.

The Biden administration's obdurate opposition to face reality in domestic as well as foreign policy matters has already caused enormous disarray worldwide. The reign of reason has been overthrown in the federal government. The seeds of catastrophic defeat have already been sown in the current administration's failures to resolve deep-rooted and more recent conflicts in American society. More significantly, President Biden is definitely personally incapable as well as mentally incapable of rallying the nation around his campaign and inaugural speech narratives which were designed to enable the United States of America to live up to its full potential.

One of the most important principles of democracy is election certainty. The peaceful transfer of power has been the bedrock of the American political system since its foundation. Occasionally, the outcome of elections has been disputed. However, the November 2020 elections are still being challenged in several states and counties with good reasons. Judges across the nation have been ordering repeated recounts for election irregularities and even outright fraud committed by abnormally biased persons and even criminally disposed election officials.

This totalitarian assault on American democracy has not been because of President Trump.

Since January 20, 2021, the United States of America has a new president, yet the country is even more divided over race, over values, over the future, over how to get there, over the budget, over global warming, and over foreign threats and challenges. The United States of America needed a leader. What it got last November is a demented, unhinged, and psychotic president. The sum total of President Biden's idiocy is a nation bereft of leadership because the chief executive is a doofus. Mentally incapable of differentiating between reality and irresponsibly made-up lies such as his nonexistent coal miner grandfather, his theft of Neil Gordon Kinnock's narrative about his ancestors, his countless plagiarisms from Marx, Lenin, Stalin, Mao, and other Communist personalities' sayings, President Biden clearly suffers fatal limitations on his abilities to cope with reality as it is.

Vice President Kamala Harris is no better. She is intellectually a nobody, a zero. Having been promoted in California by her so-called mentor in the Senate Willy Brown, she excelled only as a loudmouth hyper-partisan. Like her boss the president, she has exhibited traits of mental imbalance and an inability to live in reality unless it is twisted to conform with her psychopathologies which she has richly projected on friends and foes alike.

The cabinet as a whole and its secretaries are mostly incompetent and inexperienced political hacks who can only be described as useful idiots. Beginning with Fudge at HUD and continuing with Buttigieg at DOT, Granholm at Energy, Tanden at OMB, Mayorkas at DHS, Haaland at Interior, Becerra at HHS, and ending with Thomas-Greenfeld at the UN, Gardona at Education, and Raimondo at Commerce, the most charitable characterization could be that President Biden's cabinet is diverse. Thus, instead of a unifier and a healer with the magic touch, the majority of the American voters presumably elected a severely mentally handicapped person who exists in a double Orwellian and Kafkaesque trap.

As a result, the Biden administration is buried under an avalanche of crises, stretching from the economy to the financial system as well as the discombobulated energy policy to chaos and anarchy at the southern border and beyond to China, Russia, Afghanistan, and the Middle East, via Iran. As Tim Murtaugh suggested in the *Federalist*, in his article titled "All Biden Needed To Not Screw Up The Presidency Was Stay In His basement, And He Failed," President Biden "has badly mismanaged things, contributing to a cluster of problems that are increasingly spiraling out of control." The April 2021 employment numbers were hugely disappointing, and unemployment rose to 6.1 percent. The cyber attack on the Colonial Pipeline coupled with mixing "social justice" with the stopping of the Keystone XL pipeline while blessing the Nord Stream 2 pipeline from Ust-Luga, Russia, to Lubmin near Greifswald, Germany, and indulging his administration in raising the national debt to almost $30 trillion with wholesale tax hikes will surely end in an economic and financial disaster. The tax hikes are coupled with rising inflation foreshadowing a major political backlash against the Biden administration's destructive incompetence.

President Biden's multiple plans to restart the economy are poorly thought out and fundamentally clueless. Some are even outrightly racist and thus illegal. As Betsy McCaughey reported in *Real Clear Politics* on May 26, 2021, "The Biden administration is poised to hand out billions of dollars to what it misleadingly labels 'socially disadvantaged' farmers, restaurateurs, and other business owners hurt by the pandemic." Whites are excluded from receiving any monies from President Biden's American Rescue Plan, presumably because they are not recognized by his administration as Americans. Only Blacks, American Indians, Alaskan Natives, Asians, Hispanics, and Pacific Islanders qualify as real Americans. So much for national unity. So much for healing the soul of the nation. And so much for President Biden's leadership qualities. As Betsy McCaughey rightly noted, "The U.S. Constitution forbids discrimination based on race."

Anyway, throwing money that the United States of America does not have at the economy that does not need it to that extent will certainly make the deficit much worse. His tax hikes will only hurt individuals as well as the economy, and according to Joshua Jahani of Jahani and Associates, they "are unlikely to yield the windfall Biden expects." As a result, the current $28.2 trillion national debt will exponentially rise even faster. To add insult to injury, when all of the unfunded liabilities are included in the balance sheet as private companies are legally required to do, the national debt already exceeds $120 trillion. Although the Biden administration treats the national debt cavalierly, economist David Andolfatto noted in a recent article prepared for the Federal Reserve Bank of St. Louis that the markets and not the government decide how much debt is bearable, "There is presumably a limit to how much the market is willing or able to absorb in the way of Treasury securities for a given price level (or inflation rate) and a given structure of interest rates. However, no one really knows how high the debt-to-GDP ratio can get. We can only know once we get there."

In comparison, the tipping point of Greece's debt to its GDP was 129 percent at the end of 2020. The U.S. debt-to-GDP ratio in May 2021 is nearly a third larger than the entire U.S. economy. This ratio is measurably higher than Greece's debt-to-GDP ratio in 2010, when it received a bailout from the International Monetary Fund to avoid defaulting on its obligations.

Going back in time, books trying to answer the question of why Rome failed have filled libraries. Ludwig von Mises found the answer in the Roman Empire's rejection of individual creativity and free markets, "The marvelous civilization of antiquity perished because it did not adjust its moral code and its legal system to the requirements of the market economy." For good measure, he added, "A social order is doomed if the actions which its normal functioning requires are rejected by the standards of morality, are declared illegal by the laws of the country, and are prosecuted as criminal by the courts and police. The Roman Empire crumbled to dust because it lacked the spirit of [classical] liberalism and free enterprise. The policy of interventionism and its political corollary, the Fuhrer Principle, decomposed the mighty empire as they will by necessity always disintegrate and destroy any social entity." President Biden, his advisors, and their extremely radical followers should take note. According to Ludwig von Mises, ideologies hostile to the spirit of liberty and aggressively promoting totalitarianism as a panacea for social justice and equity have always destroyed what they pretended to save.

Proof that President Biden has not learned from universal or American history or the presently existing deep fragmentation of the nation is his newest action to further divide the American people. As CNN reported on May 23, 2021, "President Joe Biden will mark the solemn anniversary of George Floyd's death this week by hosting Floyd's family at the White House, giving the President a fresh chance to pressure lawmakers on Capitol Hill to reach an agreement on police reform legislation." Using George Floyd, a hardened and ruthless criminal, to appease the most idiotic wing of the Democrat Party, President Biden has given the seal of presidential approval to the long-term suicide of the Black community. Furthermore, by making George Floyd a positive example of acceptable Black behavior while one-sidedly condemning the police in general, President Biden has practically glorified Black lawlessness and promised impunity from criminal acts only for Black people.

Nothing can be more destructive than such an idiotic act against the rule of law and the great civilization of the United States of America. It's true that the Black community in America has been bleeding from many self-inflicted wounds, including the disintegration of the majority of Black families, the resulting absence of fathers in the lives of more than 70 percent of the Black youth, the victimization of the Black population in general by the unconscionable Democrat Party, and the existence of poor leadership. Under these circumstances, collapse is inevitable, and no amount of money or abundance of slick rhetoric can change the negative trajectory of Black existence. Finally, the deep past history of the Black community in Africa, Europe, and the United States of America has proven that adhering to the convenient but fallacious narrative of victimhood has been unfailingly marked by recurring failures.

Unequivocally, President Biden, his administration, and both Houses of Congress with their slim majorities have embarked on a disastrous zigzag course seeking to combine ill-conceived reforms and totalitarian control by the federal government. The president's executive orders, his appointments, and the growing influence of the most extreme radical elements of the Democrat Party have become a sure receipt of short-, mid-, and long-term disasters for the Democrats and their supporters. Confined to his new "basement" in the White House, President Biden lives for the day. Obviously lacking wisdom, perspective, and vision, President Biden has been an unmitigated disaster internationally as well.

In foreign affairs, reopening the American Consulate in East Jerusalem, restoring aid to the Arab population in Gaza, and reviving President Obama's disastrous Iran policy while bashing the Abraham Accord as a failure but declaring full support for Israel all demonstrate the lack of coherent foreign policy on the part of the Biden Administration. Adding insult to injury, heavy business involvements by President Biden personally as well as his family with the extremely corrupt regimes in Russia, China, and Ukraine while being private citizens have made a mockery out of his media-projected image of an honest individual. In reality, his and his family's history of corruption renders his ability to represent American national interests well greatly questionable and extremely suspect.

Having surrounded himself exclusively with failed Obama courtiers and bereft of the ability to enforce his will, President Biden lives not just in a vacuum but also dying a slow death in his politically miserable cul-de-sac. Meanwhile, the world is watching. Presidents, prime ministers, and politicians of every persuasion throughout the world either ogle with unabashed glee or stare with worrying sadness at the macabre political struggles in Washington, D.C.

The People's Republic of China and the Russian Federation are overreaching in their naked expansionism because they know about the weak character and lack of sanity in President Biden's thinking as well as his judgment. Collectively, the European Union and its member states have hesitantly started to oscillate between these two increasingly assertive powers. Fiddling like the Emperor Nero over his imagined universe and reality, President Biden is unaware of the possible results of his catastrophic domestic and foreign policies.

The Islamic Republic of Iran leads the Biden administration by the nose exactly the same way they did with the community organizer and internationally incompetent Barack Obama. The states in the Near and Great Middle East are desperately trying to save their relative domestic stabilities amidst the relentless expansionist designs of Beijing, Moscow, Ankara, and Tehran. The states of the Asian continent and Australia are becoming increasingly nervous about the reckless encroachment of the People's Republic of China on their individual as well as collective sovereignty. Without American leadership, the world is gradually becoming a despotism of rumors and the totalitarianism of lies.

Finally and most recently, there is Afghanistan. Referring to President Biden's "accomplishments in office," Victor Davis Hanson remarked at American Greatness, "Almost everything Joe Biden has touched since entering office has turned to dross." Explaining the reason for this Doofus-in-Chief's utter failure, he opines that Biden is just a "cardboard cutout, a garden-variety Democratic Party hack" who "has no clue about the actual destructive implementation of his toxic policies." Calling him a "rank opportunist" who is riding woke leftism as "the country's new trajectory," aiming "to ram down a hard-left agenda in the fashion of a torpedo that itself blows up when it hits the target," Victor Davis Hanson concludes that President Biden is an idiot.

Clearly, the Afghan withdrawal debacle has demonstrated the dangers posed by this demented president to the American nation and its political culture. In my article "Afghanistan—The Graveyard of American Political Culture," I concluded that the glaring and ubiquitous incompetence coupled with the idiotic Wokiesm that has permeated the minds of establishment Democrats made this Doofus-in-Chief exchange reality for a pie in the sky, "Demented Joe, his incompetent administration, and all those responsible for the utterly botched withdrawal, must go! After that, the American people must wise up and finally begin to create a competent and accountable civil service in place of a power-hungry federal bureaucracy."

7

The Path to National Harmony

DUE TO THE naivete and inherent goodness of the majority of the American people, the overall situation across the nation is growing more and more alarming. From the doubts about the incorruptibility of the November 2020 elections, the exponentially widening lawlessness accompanied by political, economic, and moral decline, and the striking inertia of the Biden administration as well as the Democrat-controlled and ideologically driven Congress, the United States of America is in danger of being transformed into a one-party totalitarian Stalinist state. Moreover, the growing constitutional crisis is beginning to erode the faith of the people in the core institutions of the Republic. Finally, the disgraceful and aggressive politicization of written, electronic, and social media with their biased and unsubstantiated news services is literally murdering the free flow of objective information with unsubstantiated lies. Ubiquitous corruption financed by politically immature CEOs across a broad range of businesses are dangerously approaching that of many formerly failed empires in history.

Clearly, the lessons of the Egyptian and Persian Empires, the self-destruction of the Greek city states, specifically Athens and

Sparta, the overindulgence of Rome, the disunity of the Holy Roman Empire, the overextension of Spain and Portugal, the primitive administration of the Tsarist Russia with its oversized continental ambitions, and the catastrophic global designs of Mussolini's Italy and Hitler's Germany as well as the arrogance of Imperial Japan in the 20th century are being forgotten in Washington, D.C.

It appears that idiocy is not an isolated sickness, rather it has been a recurring intellectual pandemic throughout history. Running the entire world had never been successful. On the contrary, trying to manage the rest of the world's affairs has always led to the inevitable collapse of empires that undertook this impossible task. Therefore, with the end of the United States of America's longest war in its history in Afghanistan, its aim of the Jewish equivalent of "Tikkun Olam" must come to an end. However, this does not mean that the United States of America should not strive for a world in which the present and future generations live better.

True, intolerance and even hatred are not only American characteristics but also universal traits of rulers and elected politicians. Indeed, intolerance and hatred are twin cancers that have shattered nations as well as mighty empires. Combined, they always cause political, economic, financial, and cultural suicide by having rejected domestic tranquility and international moderation. Having demanded unconditional allegiance, all previous empires have devoted their resources to expansionist and even genocidal goals.

Presently, the Democrat Party and its domestic terrorist organizations, such as Black Lives Matter, Antifa, and the multitude of race-based groups, are demanding absolute power and money from the majority while promoting a vague Black historical identity in order to destroy the constitutional order, democracy, and rule of law in the United States of America. Their foundational principles are extreme violence, murder, mayhem, and lawless destruction in the name of Black victimhood. Their war on behalf of the rule of Black identity in turn begs the question, do Blacks have a unique Black identity that has been based on a unique culture and civilization? How would creating a domestic-terrorist-run government serve the interests of societal harmony of the American people?

Inherently, Blackism exclusively means the violent and racist rejection of "White supremacy." This single focus on totalitarianism by a miniscule minority is aggravatingly negative. Black Lives Matter leaders, especially its founders and their like-minded political supporters in Congress as well as state and city governments, reject 'Whiteness" and promote domestic terrorism based on racism on steroids. While having no ideas or detailed programs about their new Black totalitarian state, their sole battle cry has been, "Kill White supremacy." Black gangs who have attacked Whites, burnt entire cities, blocked roads, occupied entire city blocks, and intimidated the population have been bragging about being "Armies of Liberation."

President Biden's idiotic overindulgence in providing monies to perpetuate the workless orgy of unemployment benefits will only expand the development and preservation of the idea that claiming victimhood can indeed be a very profitable way of life. However, throwing good money after bad is exactly the reason preventing any lasting resolution of the ethnic and racial conflicts in America since 1964. As a consequence, the Doofus-in-Chief in the White House merely perpetuates the conflict by preventing any real solution to these conflicts. On the contrary, President Biden's welfare-based solutions for the so-called "inequities" will only breed further violence and domestic terrorism.

Not being content with perpetuating racial hatred domestically, a recently leaked State Department cable by an inside source was published on May 24, 2021, by *Human Events News* and sent out to all American embassies by Secretary Antony Blinken. This cable informed them that "the Department supports the use of the term 'Black Lives Matter' in messaging content, speeches, and other diplomatic engagements with foreign audiences to advance racial equity and access to justice on May 15 and beyond (italics added). We encourage posts to focus on the need to eliminate systematic racism and its continued impact."

The cable memorandum went on to say, "This cable constitutes a blanket written authorization for calendar year 2021 from the Under Secretary for Management (M) to display the BLM flag on the external-facing flagpole to any Chiefs of Mission who determine such a display is appropriate in light of local conditions." The full text of the original cable memorandum was reproduced by the paper. This memorandum is not worth the paper that it was written on. It is simply political garbage dressed up as bureaucratic virtue.

The entire content of the cable memorandum is loaded with anti-American hatred and treasonous lies about George Floyd and Black Lives Matter. By presenting the United States of America to the world as an inherently racist country and demanding racial equity and social justice for Blacks, the Biden administration's agenda is focused on and committed to destroying America. Almost the entire cable memorandum's content is devoted to this anti-American objective and remains the foundation for President Biden's extremely radical political culture and lawlessness.

In this sense, Blackism is nothing but misconstrued identity politics designed to cause all Blacks to believe that they are the miserable victims of "White supremacy." Propagating the death of a hardened criminal as injustice and promoting a domestic terrorist organization as legitimate begs the question, is President Biden, Vice President Harris, and members of his administration not understanding that legitimizing criminality and terrorism does not serve the interests of peace as well as the unity of the nation and the future of the Black minority? Do these same public servants not comprehend that Black Lives

Matter means only one thing—the rejection of the United States of America in any form? And moreover, do they not realize that the calls for "equity" and "social justice" are irredeemably negative notions? Can they really not see that focusing on destruction rather than a positive self-definition sacrifices the Black minority's future on the altar of their surreptitious political ambitions? Unquestionably, were it not for the Democrat Party, there would be no "systematic and institutionalized racism" today in the United States of America. The problem is not racism that does not exist but the barefaced mendacity of the Democrat Party.

To substantiate the utter idiocy of President Biden and his administration, it will suffice to quote verbatim the statement by Charge d'Affaires Marc Dillard on May 25, 2021, in Budapest, Hungary, "Today, we commemorate the one-year anniversary of the murder of George Floyd by a police officer in Minnesota. We recognize the United States' long history of racism, and we recommit to the unfinished work of fighting racial injustice at home. The protests that took place last year across the world, including in Hungary, remind all of us that racism and xenophobia are global problems. By standing together against hate, discrimination, and intolerance wherever they occur, we can together honor George Floyd's legacy and help build a more just and equal future for all."

The comments that came by the dozens from average Hungarians are also worthy to be quoted verbatim. Ms. Virag Garboczi expressed her opinion in English, "What a BS propaganda pusher the embassy site became since the new retard took office for the bankrupt corporation in D.C.! Judgement day is coming." Theo Basch also expressed his opinion in English, "Thank you guys for further deteriorating the position of most USA expats in Hungary. Yes, it was a cable from State but it was optional. Just makes our life harder. I am not a racist. And if anyone at the embassy is, they should study the CRT or see '13' and get worse. Been here for 31 years. Never felt so let down." Mr. Zsolt Varkonyi said in Hungarian, "George Floyd is a criminal drug dealer who committed violent crimes against defenseless women. To present him as a victim is grotesque and brazen insolence against the real victims of violence in the USA."

Daniel Lebeau stated, "Are you guys going to be flying the BLM Marxist flag as well?! What a sham honoring a despicable piece of scum in any way, shape and form! The truth is coming...judgment day shall soon be upon us all, there's no escape! #AZ audit; GAaudit; #Back The Blue; #Military Tribunals; #NurembergCode." Mr. Pal Odon had this reaction in Hungarian, "We fought against Marxism that attacked from the East. And now the West wants to force us to do it." Martha Garza said in English, "What a bunch of crap." Mr. Imre Woth stated in Hungarian, "Excuse me, but this man is a criminal and heavy recidivist. He resisted the police and could have been dangerous in his drugged condition. The policeman followed protocol. [...] He died because of his health condition. [...] Strange that the USA raises a sorry case to the level of an international problem.

Asking who provide[s] protection for the policeman's family and the protection of all those who were murdered by the lynching mob in the name of democracy?"

Not a single supporting reaction. Only negative and condemning comments. On the other hand, the Biden administration is presented in its worst. The president is also the Anti-American-in-Chief now. As it turns out, he is convinced that his most important mandate is to incite hatred against the United States of America globally. Without question, he is the most despicable un-American on earth.

As the Preamble of the Constitution states, "We the People." A nation is the sum of its people regardless of race, ethnicity, religion, and origin. In a democracy, the majority of the people decide who their elected representatives shall be. Although President Biden and Vice President Harris are in office now, they do not represent the majority of Americans. What they represent is a small minority dedicated to destroying liberty and replacing it with a totalitarian Stalinist dictatorship.

The "We the People" absolute also means that elected public servants are obligated to tell the truth and nothing but the truth to the people. Forced to conceal the truth because of their lying agendas, President Biden and his administration continuously deceive those who elected them on false promises and misleading policy declarations. Precisely as Adolf Hitler instigated World War II for ideological reasons, including his belief that he and the German race were designated to save humanity from the

Jews, the domestic terrorists assembled under the flags of Black Lives Matter, Antifa, and other like-minded terrorist organizations think they are fighting to annihilate the White race in order to save all the Blacks across the globe.

If not decisively stopped, the Democrat Party's intention to normalize this bigotry and hatred will have profound implications for generations to come in the United States of America and beyond. As economies throughout the world are struggling to recover from the devastating effects of the pandemic, as unemployment has become a major political challenge, as anti-government sentiments are reaching critical levels, hatred and anti-Americanism are unbelievably fueled by the elected government of the United States of America. This poisonous multiplication of negative attitudes provides a fertile ground for the spread of thoughtless extremism, just as it did in the first half of the 20th century.

For these reasons, "We the People" must understand that what has been happening in their country under the deceptive guise of "Racial Equity" is nothing but a process for destroying American civilization, culture, and future progress. They must be reminded of Winston Churchill's refusal to appease Adolf Hitler. In his uncompromising policies, he was fortified by his conviction that the United States of America stood by him as the mighty guarantor of Western civilization. He also held that everyone, regardless of his or her race, ethnicity, or religion, had a solemn duty to present and future generations to protect this civilization with all of his or her might. Thus, no matter their origin, race, ethnicity, or religion, the American people as a nation must unyieldingly and unflinchingly defend the most democratic civilization in world history.

To fail in this obligation will certainly mean the long reign of totalitarianism, barbarism, chaos, and anarchy around the world. Finally, "We the People " across the globe must comprehend that the present neo-racism of the Democrat Party and the various Black organizations possesses a vile and barbaric pseudo-belief that violently rejects Western civilization in its entirety. As Hitler believed in the superiority of the German "Herrenvolk," so does neo-racism declare the superiority of the Black race over all other races, even including Native Americans, Caribbeans, Polynesians, Asians, Arabs, and Hispanics.

Realistically, there are two Americas in 2021. The false legend of the 1619 Project, the misrepresentation of slavery, and the varnishing of the United States of America's whole history have only been adopted by the Democrat Party when President Trump decisively beat the hapless and incompetent Hillary Rodham Clinton. The global resistance to President Trump's policies, including the Lincoln Project, has shown the extent of base hypocrisy of those who have been dedicated to do the work of the anti-American horde at home as well as abroad.

More ominously, this anti-American resistance has taken a decidedly radical left-wing character, especially after the spread of the COVID-19 pandemic. The violent nature of 2020 has meant that the ideological cultural war has taken a dangerously uncompromising character, leading to extreme violence, mayhem, and ubiquitous distraction. In this development and with the most supreme irony, the Democrat Party and its political proxies allied themselves with the People's Republic of China and effectively with the Russian Federation against the United States of America. As a consequence, the divide between the hostile minority and the patriotic majority has further widened. With the dubious election victory of Joe Biden, this separation has grown even more catastrophic. President Biden is mentally sick and has visibly become the prisoner of the radical left's lies and illusions, descending into degenerate ideological denials and political nihilism.

Indeed, the present condition of the country is grave. In this crucial situation, it is the duty of every patriotic American to save the United State of America's greatness and honor. It is their responsibility to restore and preserve the glory of America in its dynamic past, in its steadily improving present, and in its global promise of the future. As President Reagan said in his October 27, 1964, speech in Los Angeles, "You and I have a rendezvous with destiny. We'll preserve for our children this, the last best hope of man on earth, or we'll sentence them to take the last step into a thousand years of darkness." Paraphrasing his answer, Americans must also decide whether "We the People" are ready to take back their sovereignty or whether they will surrender their absolute power to a miniscule mob of hate-filled and blood-thirsty idiots.

They must assert themselves and fight resolutely to protect the real American Revolution from those who want to kill it.

But how to defend the United States of America, and how to fight the cancer of Black racism? First, Americans must counter the fallacious and insidious narratives of Black Lives Matter, Antifa, and the Democrat Party with all their might. Americans must demand that the same standards should apply for Blacks and their supporters as they so loudly and hypocritically insist upon for all others, especially Whites.

Second, Americans must abandon overplaying their natural inclination of empathy toward the less fortunate. In this context, Americans must understand that these domestic terrorists are determined to annihilate the constitutional order of the United States and replace it with a totalitarian despotism of a miniscule minority.

Third, Americans must reject the race-based extremist "progressivism" that preaches using force is the monopoly of Blacks but forbidden even in its legal form by non-Blacks.

Fourth, Wokeism's teachings that everything which is non-Black is "White supremacy" and that Blacks are "victimized people of color" must be rejected because such arguments distort reality and contribute nothing to the stability and tranquility of the nation.

Fifth, the fallacious comparison between "good Blacks" and "evil Whites" must be exposed for what it is—namely, false and artificially manufactured neo-racist filth.

What needs to be done? First, Americans must rise up and express their utter disgust about these neo-racist sentiments in no uncertain terms. Second, Americans must demonstrate that no one is a victim in American democracy, only those who want to shamelessly benefit from claiming victimhood. In this context, the overwhelming majority must show strength and act accordingly. Third, Americans must never apologize for defending their country against these domestic terrorists whose sole objective is to destroy it. Fourth, history matters. Americans must not let these uneducated and hate-filled anti-American idiots get away with their self-serving and absolutely false narratives. In this respect, Americans must emphasize their generosity toward minorities in general and Blacks in particular. Moreover, Americans must unequivocally state that they strive for justice, peace, and harmony within the nation. This desire and intent must be repeated over and over again.

Equipped with the certainty of representing the truth, Americans must not be afraid to express their pride in their country's glorious history, admirable present, and promising future. Only the United States of America, certain in its self-confidence and its citizens' determination to fight the evil of neo-racism, can maintain its position as a "Shining City upon a hill" for the rest of the world.

www.ingramcontent.com/pod-product-compliance
Lightning Source LLC
Chambersburg PA
CBHW031428270326
41930CB00007B/614